# Ask Me Smarter!

Brain Questions for Kids that are FUN-da-men-tal
In Helping Them SOAR to Scholastic Success

MATH

## Preschool – 5th Grade

By: Donna M. Roszak

**Ask Me Smarter!**

Brain Questions for Kids that are FUN-da-men-tal in Helping Them SOAR to Scholastic Success

MATH

Preschool – 5<sup>th</sup> Grade

Published in the United States by: Zebra Print Press, LLC

Cover Design by Donna M. Roszak
Cover Creation by www.jimandzetta.com
Interior layout and typesetting by www.jimandzetta.com
Ebook conversion by www.jimandzetta.com

Library of Congress Control Number: 2017911083

ISBN: 978-0-9860801-0-4 (Trade Paperback)
       978-0-9860801-4-2 (Hard Cover)

Printed in the United States of America

First Edition

Website: **www.askmesmarter.com**

*To my son Lucas who has always believed in this book and is my biggest supporter, to my mother Dorothy, whom I hope would be proud, and to my-mother-in law Joan who has continued to encourage me throughout this endeavor.*

# Table of Contents

# A Note to Parents, Guardians, and Teachers

This book is based on the premise that parents/guardians are their children's greatest and most influential teachers!

This book is designed as a one-source tool to help parents/guardians empower their children with a solid knowledge foundation, *based on traditional state content standards per grade level*, as they progress through their elementary school years. It is intended to enhance and reinforce the facts, ideas, and concepts that children are learning in school. This book serves to take away the guesswork, and to provide concrete questions that relate to the listed content standards per grade level. It is an oral approach to disseminating primarily rote information. It is a book based on the notion that learning is a life-long process, and that children learn differently and at different rates. Leaning is not always aligned with chronological age. It is a book that is sensitive to the fact that children come from diverse cultural upbringings and have diverse educational backgrounds and experiences.

**What it is NOT**: This book is *not* a school curriculum guide. It is *not* intended to be a quiz, a trivia game of random questions, or a competition venue. It is *not* a school textbook or workbook. It is *not* a manual for homeschoolers. It is *not* intended to be a substitute for fulfilling all school grade objectives and outcomes. It is *not* intended to promote the higher level thinking skills as outlined in Bloom's taxonomy. Further, it is *not* expected that children memorize and "master" all questions at any given grade level before proceeding to the next.

Knowledge gained by answering *Math* content questions is a sound learning strategy in that it is:

**S**pecific
**M**easurable
**A**ttainable
**R**esults oriented
**T**ime framed by grade level
**E**mpowering
**R**einforcing

# Preface

This book provides a **one-source** guide for parents/guardians/teachers to help their children learn important **MATH** facts and concepts across the elementary levels that are child, grade, and age appropriate. All the grade levels are integrated together into one book to achieve a comprehensive approach that also accommodates different learning paces. It further allows for review and reinforcement based on child-readiness and retention capacity. Even though a child may learn one topic in one year does not guarantee the child will retain that same information and have the retention and recall capacity to build on that knowledge the following school year!

This oral approach is based on the premise that knowledge is acquired through the senses: sight, hearing, touch, smell, and taste. The more senses that are used in learning, the higher the retention rate will be. Children have different learning rates and different learning styles. If "speaking" is added to hearing and seeing, the learning will come even faster, and retention will be maximized. It can be concluded then, that learners have a higher retention of what they HEAR, and SAY than by what they *SEE* alone. Employing more than one sense in learning then, as this book aims to do, is what makes the learning permanent. When all is said and done, the key to long-term retention is sustained practice over time.

This book also provides a vacation or summer "bridge" tool for young learners when school is not in session. "Ask Me Smarter" may also prove to be a good companion during a long road trip!

Inherent in this simple question format is building a child's self-esteem with a *low-anxiety* verbal approach, empowering him or her with essential knowledge, facts, and insights.

This book is a result of my difficulty in comprehending my son's just published 5th grade social studies textbook that was so convoluted with facts and minute details that the understanding of the main idea was completely lost. After reading a particularly wordy passage on the Civil War, my son had no clue from that reading which leader was on which side and who ultimately won the war! It further stems from my frustration in locating a resource that did not read like a textbook, or one that was not specific to just one grade level or operate like a workbook. Further, many libraries and bookstores have an abundant selection of educational psychology books, how-to books, science experiment books, how to read books, colorful trivia decks, but I was not able to locate a single resource that provides a direct and comprehensive approach to asking specific questions to young learners across all core and non-core disciplines. Trivia cards and interactive websites while fun and educational, are somewhat random and hit or miss with regard to ensuring coverage of essential facts encompassing all the necessary academic subject areas. I felt compelled to write something that might help fill a niche I felt was lacking, and one that expands on current resources. To this end, it was my intent to compile several grade levels into one book.

# How to Use This Book

It is important to use careful judgment in ascertaining which topics and how many questions should be asked of your child (children) at any one time. It is encouraged that questions be asked from different topics and questions that encompass different grade levels as appropriate. For example, a 1st grader may benefit from being posed "2nd grade" questions as well as being asked questions from the "kindergarten" section on any given topic. A 5th grader would similarly benefit from being asked a 3rd grade question! Some overlap with regard to the questions should be expected. Further, it is important to note that what may be deemed a "2nd grade" question in one state, may be regarded as a "3rd grade" question in another. In addition, some topics may be listed as a content standard in one state and not another. The question, "Why do you save money?" is posed as a pre-school question. That same question can be asked at any grade level. Theoretically, the older and more knowledgeable the child, the higher the level of response.

**Core Questions**: It is given that many questions in this book could represent a full week lesson, many worksheets, practice, application, and analysis. In many cases, a choice is offered after a question, but this choice could easily be eliminated if need be, or if the question is asked for the second or third time.

**MATH**: These questions serve as a representation of common math topics introduced during the formative years. Math has an inherent challenge as a child's level understanding increases. Some questions may prove difficult in a question format, especially in the later elementary grades. Allowing for paper and pencil computation, and actually *looking* at the math questions should be encouraged if need be.

**IMPORTANT**: It should not be expected that children *master* a grade level before proceeding to the next! The emphasis is on the questions, *not* the grade level. As both a mother and an educator, one of the best pieces of advice I ever received was, "teach the child, not the grade or subject."

Questions are somewhat sequential and are inherently progressive as students gain knowledge. The questions are aimed to serve as a *representation* of what is listed as the prescribed "standards" or learning outcomes for the elementary grade levels in most states.

Parents/guardians/teachers are encouraged to *re-word* questions, repeat questions, and improvise. For example, if on one occasion you ask your child: "What is the opposite of "*less than*?" Next time ask, "What is "*greater than*" the opposite of?"
Further, many questions have an inherent challenge in that they are posed with a choice, something that can, and should be omitted at the discretion of the interrogator.

If questions are asked at bedtime, an ideal time for the brain to process information and store it for future retrieval, ask your child some of the **same** questions the next morning for further reinforcement and empowerment. If the question has a choice of two or more answers, leave out the choice when asking the question again.

Some questions listed as curriculum content standards will and should illicit further discussion. Many questions may be posed as yes and no or true and false questions, simply to suggest a specific learning objective. For many of the questions it is suggested that *similar* types of questions be asked to promote further competence and awareness. For example, a preschooler may be asked to name something **large** in his or her bedroom. You can follow up with, "What is found in nature that is *large*? A high level question posed may ask the learner to name all numbers *greater than* 5 and *less than* 15.

The intention of the author is for this book to be used as an oral and auditory approach to learning and reviewing or discussing information, but it certainly would work well for a learner to read the questions and see how many questions he or she can answer correctly. It is intended to enhance and compliment what our children are already learning in school or at home. Its all-inclusive format and oral approach is what makes it unique, I believe.

If a child seems intrigued by a particular question or answer, I would highly encourage seeking out other resources from books, the Internet, pictures, etc. (See list of further resources.) We need to expand upon our children's great capacity to learn and feed their unwavering curiosity!

My hope is that your child will be engaged and challenged, and therefore empowered through this oral questioning format.

In assessing correctness, the answers are located in the appendix in numerical order.

**Further Resources**:
Library (School and Local)
Internet
Family Members
Field Trips
Field Experts
Authentic Learning Moments (Teaching fractions while cutting and serving pizza)
Real-time applications: (Conduct a science experiment: What time of day is your shadow longer; shorter? Follow a recipe.)
"Wonder" Questions (What do you wonder about?)
Have your child ask YOU a question! If you are unable to answer it, suggest that you seek out the answer together.

It needs to be stated that information expands exponentially every day. Any given topic in and of itself could easily fill a library. One war may be an entire semester of study at the University level! Neither an entire library, nor the nearly infinite information capacity of a computer could ever fit into one manageable book. Given the limits and constraints of time and space, the inclusion of any topic or question is frequently at the expense or exclusion of another. If I was remiss in any regard, I invite the reader to fill in any perceived missing questions, as you deem appropriate. What follows is a compilation of questions that encompass a wide array of essential knowledge questions aimed at children 12 and under based on traditional state learning standards. The questions loosely "cover" the learning objectives listed under the curriculum guidelines for each respective grade level. Variations and expanding upon the questions is encouraged and expected.

There is definite overlap between grade levels. Because this is a question format, this approach in no way is intended to promote and develop a mastery of grade-level *skills* (socialization, cooperative learning, reading, writing, spelling, vocabulary acquisition, story-telling etc.) Nor can this format measure a child's proficiency with technology and research skills that are an integral part of learning outcomes per grade level. Any omission or perceived bias is completely unintentional. Ideally, this question and answer approach will serve to empower our children with essential and meaningful knowledge through these fact-based questions, and provide them with a strong foundation as they continue to learn, grow, and prepare for higher learning. In so doing, our children will become informed citizens and future contributing members of our global community.

Research shows that children learn in different ways and at different rates. This book is formatted to compliment the brain networks that play a key role in learning. The "Spacing Effect" is a sound strategy in that facts are learned best when they are studied at frequent intervals over a long time span. Long-term retention of facts and information is maximized through repeated retrieval. "Ask Me Smarter" aims to provide the opportunity for optimal learning to occur in that the emphasis is on the knowledge, not the grade level.

**As you use this book as a supplemental learning tool, it is important to keep in mind:**

1) Many learners may certainly benefit from *seeing* the questions and/or working out the math problems on paper or on a calculator.

2) Many of the questions, especially in grades 3, 4, and 5 have a choice of answers after the colon. The degree of difficulty is inherent in these questions in that the choice can be read or not, at the discretion of the person asking the questions, and the readiness of the learner.

3) Many questions are yes or no questions that reflect a specific learning standard per grade level. These questions are given the answer "Yes" if only to suggest the learning goal.

4) Many of the questions asked in the higher grades are admittedly a "stretch," but they are purposely included to challenge and engage the young learner.

"Knowledge is *__potential__* power!"

*Now go ahead, ask them smarter!*

# Math

## Math – Pre-School

1.  Can you count to 10?

2.  Which number comes after 8?

3.  Which number comes before 7?

4.  Which number comes between 6 and 8?

5.  Can you count forward from 6?

6.  Can you count backward from 8?

7.  How would you complete the following sequence: 5, __, 7, 8

8.  How do we make tally marks?

9.  What songs do you know that have numbers in them?

10. What are 2, 3, 5, and 7 called because they are only divisible by 1 and itself: prime numbers or divisors?

11. Is 4 the sum or the difference in the equation 2 +2 = 4?

12. Is 1 the sum or the difference in the equation 2-1=1?

13. Can you complete a puzzle?

14. Is your stomach (piggy bank) etc. *empty* or *full*?

15. Which is *more*: 10 or 3?

16. Which has more people: a city or a family?

17. Which has *less people*: a country or a state?

18. Which is less: 7 or 2?

19. Is a basket of 5 apples more, less, or equal to a basket of 5 pears?

20. If I have two apples and you have two apples do we have more, less, or the same?

21. What is another word in math that means ***the same as***?

22. How do we say one plus one *is the same as* two?

23. What are some objects in your room that are large?

24. What are some objects in your room that are small?

25. What are some objects in your room that are blue? (etc.)

26. Can you name something that is square?

27. What is the shape of a coin, pizza, pie, button, or ring?

28. What are some objects in your room that are round?

29. What is the shape of a football field: a square or a rectangle?

30. What are some objects you can name that are in a rectangle shape?

31. What is the shape of a block?

32. Is a block similar to a cube?

33. What are some objects you can name that are square?

34. What do we call a baseball field and is another name for this shape?

35. Are hearts and stars also shapes?

36. Are spheres, cones, and prisms also considered shapes?

37. Is a diamond a shape, a type of precious stone, or both?

38. How would you continue the pattern, black, white, black, __?

39. How would you continue the pattern, red, white, blue: red, __?

40. How would you continue the pattern, pants, piano, scissors: pants,__?

41. What are the numbers in your phone number?

42. Can you tell me the numbers in your address?

43. Can you name something that is inside the house?

44. Can you name something that is outside the house?

45. Can you name something that is above the house?

46. Can you name something that is below the house?

47. Can you name something that is on top of your bed?

48. Can you name something that is under your bed?

49. Which side of the road do we drive on, the right or the left?

50. Which hand do you write with, your right hand or your left hand?

**51.**  Is the neck of a giraffe long or short?

**52.**  Is the tail on an elephant long of short?

**53.**  Is a box of feathers light or heavy?

**54.**  Is a box of tiles light or heavy?

**55.**  Which holds more: a bowl or a cup?

**56.**  Would you say that most streets are wide or narrow?

**57.**  Would you say that a path in the woods is wide or narrow?

**58.**  Which coin is a copper color and worth 1 cent?

**59.**  Which coin is a silver color and is worth 5 cents?

**60.**  Which coin is a silver color, thin, and worth 10 cents?

**61.**  Which coin is bigger than a nickel, bigger than a dime, is silver, and is worth 25 cents?

## Math – Kindergarten

62. Can you count to 100?

63. Can you count to 100 by 5's?

64. Can you count to 100 by 10's?

65. What number holds no value and is less than one?

66. Can you count forward from 7?

67. Can you count backward from 20?

68. How do you complete the following sequence, 19 _, 21, 22?

69. How many (**blue**) objects can you count in your room?

70. What number is after 7?

71. What number is before 3?

72. What number is after 79?

73. What number is between 5 and 7?

74. What is the shape of a whole pizza?

75. If a pizza is cut into 8 equal slices, and you and I eat four of the pieces, how much of the pizza is left?

76. Are four slices of an 8 piece pizza equal to half the pizza?

77. If you are sharing a big cookie with a friend, how would you divide the cookie equally?

78. Do we use measurements when we bake cookies?

79. Do we sometimes add ingredients to our cookie dough using one cup, half-cup, 1/3 cup and ¼ cup?

80. Do we measure salt and vanilla when following a recipe using teaspoons or cups?

81. Which is bigger: a tablespoon or a teaspoon?

82. When measuring ingredients for a cake is it better when following a recipe: measuring spoons or the spoons that we use for soup and cereal?

83. What is the shape of one piece of pizza or one piece of pie?

84. What is the shape of a block?

85. What is the shape of a football field?

86. What objects can you name that are round?

87. What objects can you name that are square?

88. How many sides does a square have?

89. What objects can you name that are in the shape of a triangle?

90. How many sides does a triangle have?

91. What objects can you name that are in the shape of a rectangle?

92. How many sides does a rectangle have?

93. Can you name something that is in the shape of an oval?

94. How many fingers do you have?

95. How many fingers do you have on each hand?

96. How many fingers am I holding up?

97. Can you hold up your fingers to show how old you are?

98. Can you hold up your fingers to show how ears you have?

99. Can you hold up your fingers to show how many thumbs you have?

100. Can you count backward from 10?

101. Can you count to 20 by 2's?

102. When you count by 2's, 5's or 10's is that called skip-counting?

103. Can you count to 20 by 5's?

104. Which is more 13 or 14?

105. Which is less 5 or 9?

106. What is the number that has no value?

107. What is two plus zero?

108. What is two plus two? (Use any addition facts through 10)

109. What is the sum of 5 plus 5?

110. Is 5 + 5 equal to 6+4? (Etc.)

111. Can you describe what the addition sign looks like?

112. Can you describe what the subtraction sign looks like?

113. What is 3 minus 1 equal to?

114.  What is the 10 minus 5 equal to?

115.  What is 3 minus 0? (Use any subtraction facts through 10)

116.  Can you describe what the *equals* sign looks like?

117.  How much is one penny worth?

118.  How much is one nickel worth?

119.  How much is one dime worth?

120.  How much is one quarter worth?

121.  What metal is a penny made of?

122.  Is the symbol for cent(s) the letter c with one line or two lines through it?

123.  Is the symbol for the dollar the letter "S" with one line or two lines through it?

124.  If you have eight pennies and gave me half of them, how many would I have?

125.  What is the name of the coin that is worth 5 cents?

126.  What is the name of the coin that is worth 10 cents?

127.  What is the name of the coin that is worth 25 cents?

128.  Is there a 50 cent coin?

129.  Would two quarters be equal to one half dollar?

130.  Are four quarters equal to one dollar?

131.  Is there a dollar coin?

132.  Are all coins the same size or are they different sizes?

133.  Which coin is the smallest is size?

134.  Which coin is the largest: a quarter or a 50 cent piece?

135.  How many sides does a coin have?

136.  What is the name of the side of a coin with the imprint of a president?

137.  What is the name of the other side of a coin with a picture of a building?

138.  Can you describe what the symbol for cents looks like?

139.  What is the name of our paper money?

140.  Can you describe what the symbol for dollars looks like?

141.  What are all the *red* things you can name in your room? (Classification)

142. Can you put *white* clothes in one pile and the *colored* clothes in another pile?

143. If you are making tally marks to keep track of all the red toys you have, how do you show that you have five toys?

144. What toys do you have that are big?

145. What toys do you have that are small?

146. What things are located inside a house?

147. What things are located outside a house?

148. What is located on the left side of your bed?

149. What is located on the right side of your bed?

150. What is located in the middle of your bedroom?

151. Does a boat float on the top or the bottom of a lake?

152. What part of your body is located above your neck?

153. What part of your body is located below your wrist?

154. Can you *estimate* how many stuffed animals you have?

155. Can you finish the pattern of red, blue: red _?

156. What is next in the series: white, green, pink: white _?

157. Which comes next in the pattern, dogs, turtles, cats: dogs, _?

158. What do we use to tell time?

159. How many numbers are on a clock?

160. Are there different kinds of clocks?

161. If the small hand is on the (**three**) and the big hand is on the twelve, what time is it?

162. Which tool measures length, how long something is?

163. What animals can you name that are long?

164. What animals can you name that are short?

165. What is the name of the tool for three rulers put together?

166. What is the name of the tool that tells us the temperature, or how hot or cold something is?

167. What is the name of the tool that can do math functions that has buttons that you press?

168. What is the name of the tool that tells us how heavy or light something is?

169. What animals can you name that are heavy?

170. What animals can you name that are light?

171. What object in your bedroom would be heavy and therefore hard to lift?

172. What object in your bedroom would be light and therefore easy to lift?

173. Did you come home from school in the morning, the afternoon, or the evening?

174. Did you eat breakfast before or after you got dressed today?

175. Did you brush your teeth before or after you ate supper?

176. If you are brushing your teeth after waking up, is it a.m. or p.m.?

177. What part of the day is it now?

178. What tool helps us to know the date and the time of year?

179. What are the days of the week starting with Sunday?

180. How many days are there in a week?

181. How many days are there in a month?

182. Are the number of days in a month always the same or are they different?

183. If today is Monday, what day is tomorrow?

184. If today is Thursday, what day was yesterday?

185. If today is Friday, what day is the day after tomorrow?

186. Which season comes after autumn?

187. Which season comes before spring?

188. Is the bathtub full or empty right now?

189. What do we say if we fill a glass half way with water: The glass is _?

190. What can you name that comes in pairs?

191. Can you show me what you would do if I said, "Simon Says put your *right* hand *behind* your head?

192. Can you show me what you would do if I said, "Simon Says put your *left* hand *between* your knees?

193. Can you show me what you would do if I said, "Simon Says put your *right* hand *under* your *left* foot?

194. Can you show me what you would do if I said, "Simon Says put your *left* hand beside your *right* knee?

**195.** If you are spinning a spinner that is mostly blue with a small red section, which section is the arrow most likely to point to?

**196.** Which is longer: a submarine sandwich or a bagel?

**197.** Which is shorter: a ruler or a yardstick?

**198.** Which is taller: a skyscraper or a house?

**199.** Which is lighter: a dog or an elephant?

**200.** Which container holds more: a tablespoon or a cup??

**201.** Which weighs more: a butterfly or a frog?

**202.** Which is the heaviest: a tiger, a monkey, or an elephant?

**203.** Which is the lightest: a deer, a bowling ball, or a beach ball?

## Math – 1st Grade

204. Can you count to 100 by 5's?

205. Can you count to 100 by 10's?

206. Can you count to 50 by 2's?

207. Can you count back from 10?

208. If you are counting down from 18, which number comes next?

209. If you are counting up from 49, which number comes next?

210. What number would be between zero and two on a number line?

211. Which is the faster way of counting: by 5's or by 1's?

212. What is the term for things that go together and come in two's?

213. What two separate items do you have that would be called a pair?

214. What item do you have that can be called a pair even though there is just one?

215. What is the number that represents the absence of value and comes before the number one?

216. What games do you know of that help you practice math and make it fun?

217. Do you think that there are many activities and games that you could do on the computer to help you practice math?

218. What ordinal number is the opposite of *last*?

219. Which grade comes after 1st?

220. Which grade comes before 4th?

221. Which grade comes after 9th?

222. Which grade comes before 8th?

223. What is the weather like today?

224. Can you read a thermometer?

225. What does a thermometer measure?

226. What other tools can gather information about the weather?

227. Is math important in the study of weather?

228. What are some things that fly in the air?

229. What does a kite need to move in the air?

230. What do the rotating blades of windmills create?

231. What is another word for doing something *one time*?

232. What is another word for doing something *two times*?

233. What do you get when you *double* the number 2?

234. What do you get when you *double* the number 10? (1-10, etc.)

235. What number comes next: 2, 4, 6, _?

236. What is the missing number in the following sequence: 30, _, 40, 45, 50?

237. Are the numbers 2, 4, and 6 odd or even?

238. What number comes next: 1, 3, 5, _?

239. Can you predict what number comes next: 1, 4, 7, _?

240. Are the numbers 1, 3, and 5 odd or even?

241. Is the number 23 odd or even?

242. Which even number comes after 30?

243. Which odd number comes before 50?

244. What number comes before 30? (40,50,60,70,80,90,100)

245. If a recipe calls for *2* cups of flour, and you are making a double batch of cookies, how many cups of flour would you need to add?

246. Can you name something on a stuffed animal that come in two's?

247. Can you estimate how many stuffed animals you have? (Etc.)

248. How many sides does a square have?

249. How many sides does a triangle have?

250. How many sides does a rectangle have?

251. What is the name of the shape that is round?

252. What things in our environment are round?

253. What things can you name that are in the shape of a rectangle?

254. What things can you name that are in the shape of a square?

255. What would come next in the sequence: triangle, square, triangle, _?

**256.**  What is the shape of a racetrack?

**257.**  Is a piece of ice in the shape of a cube or a sphere?

**258.**  Is the Earth in the shape of a cube or a sphere?

**259.**  Is a cube a simple shape or a solid shape?

**260.**  Are cylinders, cones and spheres solid shapes or simple shapes?

**261.**  Are points, lines, and curves simple shapes or solid shapes?

**262.**  Can you name something in the shape of a cone?

**263.**  Do you think the crescent moon in the shape of an arc is an open shape or a closed shape?

**264.**  Is a circle an open or closed shape?

**265.**  What is something you know of that is straight?

**266.**  What is something you know of that is curved?

**267.**  What are some shapes that would look different if they were turned upside down?

**268.**  What would you see if you looked through a prism?

**269.**  What are some things that might be divided in half?

**270.**  What is next in the pattern: red, green, yellow, blue: red, green _?

**271.**  Do we use less than, greater than, and equal to when we compare numbers?

**272.**  Which is greater: 60 or 70?

**273.**  Which is less: 49 or 89?

**274.**  What do say when comparing numbers: greater than, less than, equal to, or all of them?

**275.**  Is 29 greater or less than 19?

**276.**  What is another way of stating that 30 is greater than 20?

**277.**  How would you compare the numbers 25 and 25?

**278.**  Which would weigh more: one pound of feathers or one pound of stones?

**279.**  What is 0+1 (2-10)?

**280.**  What is 1+1?

**281.**  What is 2 + 2?

**282.**  What is 3+3

**283.**  What is 4+4?

**284.** What is 5+5?

**285.** What is 6 + 6?

**286.** What is 7 + 7?

**287.** What is 8 + 8?

**288.** What is 9 + 9?

**289.** What is 10 + 10?

**290.** What is 20 + 10?

**291.** What is 30 + 10?

**292.** What is 40 + 10?

**293.** What is 50 + 10?

**294.** What is 60 + 10?

**295.** What is 70 + 10?

**296.** What is 80 + 10?

**297.** What is 90 + 10?

**298.** What is the sum of 15 + 3?

**299.** What is the sum of 12 + 9?

**300.** What is the sum of 16 + 8?

**301.** Does 3 + 2 equal 2 + 3?

**302.** If 5+4=9, does 4+5=9?

**303.** Does 3 + 0 equal 0 + 3?

**304.** Is 15 + 5 greater than or equal to 10 ┃10?

**305.** Is 3 + 5 =8 the same as 5 + 3 =8?

**306.** How many dogs were walked in all if Sam walked 4 dogs and Jason walked 6 dogs?

**307.** How many pieces of furniture did the store sell if it sold 3 tables, 1 couch, and 2 chairs?

**308.** What is 9 + 2? (Basic addition facts through 9+9)

**309.** What is the missing number in the following equation: 2 + __ = 6?

**310.** What is the sign or symbol for subtraction?

**311.** What is 7-3? (Basic subtraction facts)

312. What is the difference of 18-9?

313. What is 5-2?

314. What is 10-0?

315. What is 19 +1? (29,39,49,59,69,79,89,99)

316. What is 20-1? (100,70,50,60,30,90,40,80,10)

317. What is 90-10? (80-10; 70-10, 60-10, 50-10, 40-10, 30-10, 20-10, 10-10 etc.)

318. What is 40 – 20?

319. What is 23-1-?

320. What is 17-6?

321. What is 18-9?

322. How many apples are left in the refrigerator if Ann takes 2 apples out of the drawer that has 6 apples in it?

323. How would you make 4: 8-4 or 7-2?

324. How would you make 9: 6 + 2 or 2 + 7?

325. What would come next in the pattern: 5-5=0, 4-4=0, 3-3=0, _-2=0, _ - _=0?

326. How would you continue the following sequence: 10-0=10, 10-1=9, 10-2= _, 10-3=_, 10-4=__, 10-5=_, 10-6= __, 10-7= _, 10-8= _, 10-9= _, 10-10=_?

327. Can you make a subtraction equation from the following word problem: Together Pete and Sean bought 15 bags of chips for the party. If Pete bought 8 bags, how many did Sean buy? (15 -8=__)

328. What is 90 - 60?

329. What is 50 + 40?

330. How would you complete the following: _- 3 = 6?

331. What is the related subtraction fact for **6 – 4 = 2**: 6 – 2 = 4 or 10 – 4 = 6?

332. Would you need a plus or minus sign in the following equation: 6 _ 4=10?

333. Would you need a plus or minus sign in the following equation: 10 _ 3=7?

334. In the equation 44 - 36=8, is 8 the sum or the difference?

335. Which fact is missing from the following: 5+6=11, 6+6=11, 11 - 5 = 6, __-__ = 5?

336. How many pens does Josh have all together in his supply box if he has 8 black pens and 6 blue pens?

337. What is 10 less than 31?

338. What is 10 more than 49?

339. What is the opposite of greater than?

340. What is the opposite of unequal?

341. What is the opposite of more?

342. What is the opposite of less than?

343. How would you finish the sentence using greater than, less than, or equal to: 10 is __than 8?

344. How would you finish the sentence using greater than, less than, or equal to: 6 is __than 7?

345. How would you finish the sentence using greater than, less than, or equal to: 5 is __to 5?

346. How would you finish the sentence using greater than, less than, or equal to: 82 is __than 72?

347. If Jordan has 6 stickers and Maddie has more stickers than Eli, how many stickers does Maddie have: 5 or 10?

348. What is the opposite of left?

349. What is the opposite of least?

350. Can you identify what happens to a plant as it grows?

351. What happens to the weather as we approach winter? (summer, etc.)

352. How does a person's weight change as they grow: increases or decreases?

353. Can you solve the equation: 2 + what number = 5?

354. What is the order of the following set smallest to largest (least to greatest): 22, 42, and 12?

355. What is the order of the following set largest to smallest (greatest to least): 22, 42, and 12?

356. In the number 76, which number is in the tens column? (26,36,46,56,66,86,96)

357. In the number 25, which number is in the ones column?

358. In the number 86 there are 8 tens and how many ones?

359. In the number 49, how many tens and ones are there?

360. Can you estimate: how many kids are in your class; how many dogs are in the neighborhood; how many stuffed animals you have; etc.?

361. Without looking at the clock, can you estimate what time it is?

362. What do we use to tell us the date and month of the year?

363. Do we use a calendar to plan family activities and events?

**364.** How many months are there in one year?

**365.** How many days (more or less) are in one month?

**366.** How many days are there in one week?

**367.** If today is Friday, what day was yesterday?

**368.** If today is Sunday, what day is tomorrow?

**369.** Which day comes before Saturday?

**370.** Which day comes after Tuesday?

**371.** If today is Monday, what day was the day before yesterday?

**372.** What are the two days of the weekend?

**373.** How many seconds are there in one minute?

**374.** How many minutes are there in one hour?

**375.** How many hours are there in one day?

**376.** If it is 9:00 o'clock now, what time will it be in one half hour?

**377.** Do you have a digital clock, an analog clock, or both?

**378.** When do most people go to bed: the a.m. or the p.m?

**379.** When you eat breakfast and get ready for your day, is it a.m. or p.m?

**380.** Which is the correct time unit for how long a baseball game lasts: 3 hours, 3 days, or 3 weeks?

**381.** How many eggs are there in one dozen?

**382.** Which month of the year is January: the first or the last?

**383.** If January is the first month of the year, what is the last month of the year?

**384.** What is the opposite of first?

**385.** Which month is second? (3$^{rd}$-12$^{th}$)

**386.** What grade are you in?

**387.** What grade will you be in next year?

**388.** What grade were you in last year?

**389.** What are the three months of winter in our state?

**390.** What are the three months of summer in our state?

**391.** What are the three months of autumn in our state?

**392.** What are the three months of spring in our state?

**393.** What is the name of the operation when we add things together?

**394.** What is the sign for addition?

**395.** If I have 2 books and I add 3 more, how many books do I have altogether?

**396.** How do you write the equation of 2 books and 3 more books amounts to 5 books?

**397.** What is it called when you take something away from a group?

**398.** What is the sign for subtraction?

**399.** If you have 3 books and you return 2 to the library, how many do you have left?

**400.** If you had 4 tacos on your plate but you only ate 3, what would the equation look like?

**401.** How many inches long is a ruler?

**402.** What is twelve inches equal to?

**403.** What is the name the tool that measures three feet long?

**404.** Are three feet greater than or equal to one yard?

**405.** Can we also use a tape measure tool to take measurements?

**406.** What is the correct order smallest to largest: yard, inches, and feet?

**407.** What is the appropriate unit of length of a submarine sandwich: 12 inches or 12 feet?

**408.** What is the name of the unit of measurement for distance when we drive a car or walk to school or the library?

**409.** Which tool indicates what the weight of something is?

**410.** What measurement of weight do we use: the pound or the kilo?

**411.** Which unit of weight is appropriate for a bird: 17 ounces or 17 pounds?

**412.** How much do you weigh?

**413.** If you use your hand as a measuring tool, how many hands long is your bed?

**414.** Which tool shows how hot or cold something is?

**415.** Do we in America measure the temperature in degrees Fahrenheit or degrees Celsius?

**416.** Is there another system of measurement used in many other places called the *metric* system?

**417.** What are the metric measurements for length smallest to biggest: meter, millimeter, and centimeter?

**418.** What would be the appropriate length of a spoon: 18 meters or 18 centimeters?

419. What is the metric measurement for temperature: Celsius and Fahrenheit?

420. What is the metric measurement for distance: the mile or the kilometer?

421. What is the metric measurement for weight: grams or pounds?

422. What would be an appropriate weight of a plastic bowl: 13 grams or kilograms?

423. What is the prefix "kilo" equal to: one thousand or one hundred?

424. What is the metric measurement for liquid volume: gallons or liters?

425. What are some things that are hot in temperature?

426. What are some things that are cold?

427. If you fill a gas tank in the car all the way, what do we say that the tank is: full or complete?

428. If you run out of gas, what is the tank now?

429. Can we measure solids and liquids?

430. What things can you name that are solids?

431. What things can you name that are liquids?

432. Which is bigger: a cup or a pint?

433. Which is bigger: a pint or a quart

434. Which is bigger: a gallon or a quart?

435. How would you put the following in order from smallest to largest: pint, cup, gallon, and quart?

436. What do cups, pints, quarts, and gallons all measure: liquid capacity or weight?

437. Do you typically drink ½ pint or one pint of milk?

438. In what capacity do most people buy milk that is equal to 4 quarts?

439. What are some things we might purchase by the gallon?

440. In liquid measurement, how many cups equal one pint: 2 cups or 4 cups?

441. In liquid measurement, how many cups equal one quart: 4 cups or 8 cups?

442. In liquid measurement, how many pints equal one quart: 2 pints or 4 pints?

443. In liquid measurement, how many quarts equal one gallon: 2 quarts or 4 quarts?

444. Which is greater: 7 cups or 1 quart?

445. What is the name of the unit of measurement when we fill up the tank with gas: quarts or gallons?

446. What is the name of the metric liquid measurement: a kilo or a liter?

447. If you just ate two hot dogs, would you say your stomach is empty or full?

448. If you fill the tank only half-way, would you say that it is half-full, or half-empty?

449. What would take *longer*: brushing your teeth or driving to school?

450. Which would be *shorter*: eating some grapes or eating supper?

451. If the red bag has 3 presents, the blue bag has 5 presents, and the white bag has 8 presents, which bag has the *most*?

452. If the red bag has 3 presents, the blue bag has 5 presents, and the white bag has 8 presents, which bag has the *least*?

453. If the green bag has 3 presents and the yellow bag has 3 presents, how would you compare them?

454. If you cut a round pizza into 8 slices, how many slices would make up half the pizza?

455. If you are baking cookies, might you need to have a measuring cups that measure ¼, ½, and 1 cup as you follow the recipe?

456. Is a fraction a part or a whole?

457. Is the top number of a fraction called a numerator or a denominator?

458. Is the bottom number of a fraction called a numerator or a denominator?

459. Which is greater: one-half or one-fourth?

460. Which is greater: one-third or one-fourth?

461. How many sides does a square have?

462. How many sides does a rectangle have?

463. How many sides does a triangle have?

464. Which shape does not have sides: a circle or an octagon?

465. How many sides does a hexagon have: 6 or 8?

466. How many sides does an octagon have: 6 or 8?

467. How many arms does an octopus have?

468. What red traffic sign is in the shape of an octagon?

469. Does a trapezoid resemble the shape of a skirt or a stop sign?

470. What shape would you call a globe: a sphere or a prism?

471. What shape would you call a flashlight or a soda can: a cylinder or a cube?

472. What is the shape of the crunchy part of an ice cream treat, a birthday hat, and an Indian tepee: a sphere or a cone?

473. What is the shape of a piece of ice or dice: a rectangle or a cube?

474. What shape would a piece of pie or a piece of pizza be: a sphere or a triangle?

475. What is the shape of an arc or a rainbow: a closed shape or an open shape?

476. Is a circle a closed shape or an open shape?

477. Is a straight line a shape?

478. What is it called when one part of a shape is a mirror image of the other part: symmetrical or bilateral?

479. In what direction would you make a tally mark to indicate 5 points: diagonally or straight?

480. What bar would be higher on a bar graph if one bar showed shirt sales of 40, and the other bar showed shirt sales of 32?

481. If you wanted to find out how many students wanted to go to the play, would you use tally marks or a graph to record your data?

482. How many wheels does a bicycle have?

483. How many wheels does a tricycle have?

484. How many wheels does a unicycle have?

485. What is the name of the coin that is worth 5 cents?

486. What is the name of the coin that is worth 10 cents?

487. What is the name of the coin that is worth 25 cents?

488. Is there a 50 cent coin?

489. Can you add coins together?

490. How many nickels is one dime equal to?

491. What three coins could you have that would equal one quarter?

492. What is the value of a quarter, a dime, a nickel, and a penny?

493. What is the value of one quarter and one dime?

494. What is the value of two quarters, one dime and one nickel?

495. What is the value of two quarters, two dimes, one nickel, and three pennies?

496. What are four quarters equal to?

497. What are two dimes and a five pennies equal to?

498. What are five dimes equal to?

**499.** Which coin is 25 pennies equal to?

**500.** Which coin are two dimes and a nickel equal to?

**501.** What is the value of two quarters and one dime?

**502.** If you have eight pennies and gave me half of them, how many would I have?

**503.** How many quarters are equal to one half dollar?

**504.** How many quarters are equal to one dollar?

**505.** How much money do they spend in all if Nick buys a candy bar with 5 dimes and Julia buys a candy bar with 2 quarters?

**506.** Do you have enough money if a bag of popcorn costs 25 cents and you have four nickels?

**507.** Do you have enough money if a bag of popcorn costs 25 cents and you have two dimes?

**508.** Does a person who is *bi*lingual speak one language or two?

**509.** How many languages can a person speak if he/she is *multi*lingual?

**510.** What is the probability that you will sleep in your bed tonight: certain, probable, unlikely, or impossible?

**511.** What is the probability that you will fly like a bird: certain, probable, unlikely, or impossible?

**512.** What is the probability that you will have 20 dogs: certain, probable, unlikely, or impossible?

**513.** What is the probability that you will eat breakfast tomorrow morning even though you overslept: certain, probable, unlikely, or impossible?

**514.** What letter is the Roman numeral for one?

**515.** What letter is the Roman numeral for five: V or X?

**516.** What letter is the Roman numeral for ten: V or X?

**517.** What letter is the Roman numeral for fifty: L or C?

**518.** What would Roman numeral XV be equal to?

**519.** What would Roman numeral XXX be equal to?

**520.** What would Roman numeral XIV be equal to?

**521.** What would Roman numeral LXVII be equal to?

**522.** How many total writing utensils does Jonathon have if he has 3 pens and 2 pencils?

**523.** How could you write an addition equation for the following: Rosa caught one firefly and Maya caught four, how many in all? $1 + \underline{\phantom{xx}} = \underline{\phantom{xx}}$

**524.** Do you find the range of numbers by subtracting the lowest number from the highest?

**525.** What is the range of the following numbers 10, 8, 7, 8, 6?

**526.** In the sequence 13,13,13,13,14,15 the number 13 is the one that is repeated the most, so is 13 the mode or the median?

**527.** In the numbers 5, 6, and 7, which number is the median, or the one in the middle?

## Math – 2<sup>nd</sup> Grade

**528.** Can you count to 100 by 1's?

**529.** Can you count to 100 by 20's?

**530.** Can you count to 100 by 2's?

**531.** Can you count to 100 by 5's?

**532.** Can you count to 1000 by 100's?

**533.** Can you count forward by 100's from 600: 600, _, _, _, _?

**534.** Which number is between 979 and 981?

**535.** Could Brian skip count by 5's if he begins at 20 until he reached 36?

**536.** Can you count back from 100?

**537.** How do you put 44, 25, and 33 in numerical order?

**538.** What number is missing in the following sequence: 50, _, 60, 65, 70?

**539.** What number would be next on a number line to 100: 95, 96, 97, _, 99?

**540.** Can you count forward by twos from 26: 26, _, _, _, _?

**541.** What comes next in the following pattern: yellow fish, blue fish, yellow fish, __?

**542.** What comes next in the following pattern: blue, yellow, blue; blue, yellow, yellow; blue, yellow blue; _?

**543.** Is the number 37 odd or even?

**544.** Is the number 46 odd or even?

**545.** Which of the following is an even number, 2, 3, 7, and 5?

**546.** Which odd number comes before 3, 5, 7?

**547.** Which even number comes after 2, 4, 6?

**548.** What are the ordinal numbers? (First…)

**549.** What grade are you in?

**550.** What is the abbreviation (shortened form) for first?

**551.** What is the abbreviation for second?

**552.** What is the abbreviation for third?

**553.** What is the abbreviation for fourth?

**554.** What is the abbreviation for fifth?

**555.** What is the abbreviation for sixth?

**556.** What is the abbreviation for seventh?

**557.** What is the abbreviation for eighth?

**558.** What is the abbreviation for ninth?

**559.** What is the abbreviation for tenth?

**560.** What ordinal comes after forty ninth?

**561.** Which of the following are the ordinal numbers: $50^{th}$, 40, $75^{th}$, and 66?

**562.** How is the number t-h-i-r-t-y - n-i-n-t-h written using digits? (Etc.)

**563.** How is the number t-w-o h-u-n-d-r-e-d f-o-r-t-y f-i-v-e written using digits

**564.** In the equation $4 + 2 = 6$, is 6 the sum or the difference?

**565.** In the equation $6 - 2 = 4$, is 4 the sum or the difference?

**566.** Does the following equation need a plus or a minus? $5 \_ 3 = 2$

**567.** Does the following equation need a plus or a minus? $8 \_ 4 = 12$

**568.** What is the sum of $9 + 9$?

**569.** What is $9 + 8$? ( Addition facts 0-20)

**570.** What is $12 + 13$?

**571.** What is the sum of $60 + 20$?

**572.** What is the sum of $25 + 4$?

**573.** What is the sum of $19 + 5$?

**574.** What is the sum of $73 + 13$?

**575.** What is the sum of $39 + 12$?

**576.** What is the sum of $200 + 300$?

**577.** What is the sum of $120 + 130$?

**578.** What is the sum of $6 + 7 + 3$?

**579.** What is the sum of $30 + 12 + 2$?

**580.** What is the related addition fact for $12 + 3 = 15$: $3 + \_ = \_$?

581. What is the related addition fact for $12 + 8 = 20$?

582. Which number makes the equation true: $14 + 5 = 9 + \_$?

583. What is the missing number in the equation: $830 + \_ = 839$?

584. Which number makes the equation true: $240 + 2 = 236 + \_$

585. If Lilly and Megan sold 12 regular lemonades and 6 strawberry lemonades at their lemonade stand, how many lemonades did they sell in all?

586. If the zoo has 7 adult lions and 6 baby lions how many lions are there in all?

587. If Alex made 24 cookies and Jack made 12, how many cookies did they make in all?

588. If 200 people bought blue T-shirts for the fundraiser and 150 bought red T-shirts, how many total shirts were bought: $\_ + \_ = \_$?

589. What number do you get if you double the number 20?

590. What number do you get if you double the number 25?

591. What number added to 12 would equal 20?

592. What number subtracted from 15 would give you 10?

593. What is **not** a way to make 7: 6+1; 3+4; 2+7; or 5+2?

594. What is $18 - 9$? (Subtraction facts 0-20)

595. What is the difference in 14-9?

596. What is 6-6 equal to?

597. Which is **not** a way to make 7: 7-0; 8-1; 8-0; or 10-3?

598. What is $80 - 50$?

599. What is $67 - 4$?

600. What is $21 - 7$?

601. What is $18 - 5$?

602. What is $54 - 14$?

603. What is 800-500?

604. What is 750-50?

605. What is 330-130?

606. What is the missing number in the equation: $\_$ minus one equals nine?

607. What fact is missing from this fact family: 14-2=12; 14-12 = 2; 2+12=14, __+__=___

608. Which equation does **not** equal 9: 12-2; 13-4; or 16-7?

609. What is a subtraction equation that would equal 10?

610. What number would make the equation true: 12-2 = 20 -_?

611. What is a related subtraction fact for 20 – 15 = 5: 20 - __ = __

612. What is a related subtraction fact for 30 – 10 = 20: 30 - __=__

613. If you had 14 peas and ate 8 of them, how many would be left on your plate?

614. If you had 6 Legos and needed 20 Legos to build a bridge, how many more Legos would you need?

615. How would you write a subtraction sentence for the following: Emma had 4 cookies in her lunch but two were broken and she threw them out. How many cookies does she have now: _-_=__?

616. If there are 40 pumpkins in the pumpkin patch and Lillian's class picks out 20 of them, how many are left: __ - __ = __?

617. Drew and Marcos collected 17 leaves on their walk through the woods. If Drew collected 8 leaves, how many did Marcos collect?

618. How would you balance the following equation: 9-8 = 7-_?

619. How would you balance the following equation: 239-9 = 250 - _?

620. If the total for the homerun contest was 13 and Tommy hit 8 of them, how many did Garrett hit?

621. How can you make 70: 74-4 or 69+8?

622. What is the missing number in the following: 59-9 = 4 + _?

623. If Henry and Ashlyn read a total of 22 books for the summer library reading club, and Ashlyn reads 12 of them, how many did Henry read?

624. Is 1 +17 equal to 17 + 1?

625. What number would you add to 6 to equal the sum of 3 + 7?

626. What is 55 + 0?

627. What number would you add to 4 to equal 6?

628. How many ways can you add two numbers together to make 12 besides 12+0=12? (11+1, …)

629. What is an addition sentence for the following: If Kim bought 7 cheese pizzas and Kelly bought 5 pepperoni pizzas for the party, how many pizzas did they buy in all: _+__ = _?

630. When you add zero to any number, does it change the value of that number?

631. If an input/output table reads 2 IN and 12 OUT, 6 IN and 16 OUT, what is the rule: + __?

632. Which bar would be higher on a bar graph if the bar indicating sweatshirts purchased was 25 and the bar indicating T-shirts sold was 21?

633. Can you read a pictograph?

634. Can you read a line graph?

635. What part of a Venn diagram shows the common elements of the two things being compared?

636. Is 2 greater than, less than, or equal to 3 +1?

637. Is 6 greater than, less than, or equal to 3+2?

638. Is 6 greater than, less than, or equal to 3 +3?

639. Which is greater: 76 or 67?

640. Which is less: 58 or 49?

641. Is 92 greater than, less than, or equal to 89?

642. Is 583 greater than, less than, or equal to 583?

643. In the series 1,2,5,6, which numbers are even?

644. In the series 1,2,5,6 which numbers are odd?

645. How would you continue the sequence: 22, 24, _?

646. How would you continue the sequence: 31, 33, _?

647. How would you put the following numbers in order least to greatest: 77, 71, and 70?

648. How would you put the following numbers in order greatest to least: 92, 99, and 88?

649. In the number 704, which number is in the ones column?

650. In the number 704, which number is in the tens column?

651. In the number 612, which number is in the tens column?

652. What is the value of the digit **one** in the number 16: tens or ones?

653. What is the value of the digit **eight** in the number 81: tens or ones?

654. What is the value of each digit in the number 95: _tens and _ones?

655. What is the value of each digit in the number 345: _hundreds, _tens, and _ones?

656. What is the value of each digit in the number 3,042: _thousands, _hundreds, _tens, _ones?

657. How many thousands would 300 tens be equal to: 1 or 3?

658.  Even though there are zero tens in 704, is the number zero used as a place holder?

659.  In the number 704, which number is in the hundreds column?

660.  What is the value of the digit **nine** in the number 950: hundreds or tens?

661.  What is the value of the digit **three** in the number 3,421: hundreds or thousands?

662.  How could you regroup tens and ones in the following equation: 2 tens and 22 ones = _tens and _ones?

663.  How could you regroup tens and ones in the following equation: 6 tens and 18 ones = 7 tens, and __ones?

664.  What is another way to make 65 besides 6 tens and 5 ones: 5 tens or 15 ones or 4 tens and 15 ones?

665.  Is 4 tens and 20 ones the same as 6 tens?

666.  What number is missing in the following: 6 tens and 15 ones = 7 tens and _ones?

667.  What is the sum of 300 + 20+ 9?

668.  What is the sum of 7,000 + 300 + 80 +4?

669.  In the number ten point five, is the point called a decimal point or a period?

670.  Can point five zero also be written as one half?

671.  Is point two five written as one fourth or one half?

672.  Is one point seven five written as one and seven fifths, or one and three fourths?

673.  What is the ratio if there are 20 boys in a group and 10 girls: 20:10 or 2:1?

674.  If there are 12 dogs at the pet shop and 3 cats, what is the ratio of dogs to cats?

675.  What is the term for the answer when you multiply 2 or more numbers: the product or the quotient?

676.  What is the product of 2 x 3?

677.  What is the product of 3 x 2?

678.  What is 1 x 15?

679.  When you multiply 1 by any number, does it equal that number or a higher one?

680.  What is 8 x 0?

681.  When you multiply any number by zero, does it always equal zero or the higher number?

682.  What is 5 x 5? (Multiplication facts 0-10)

683.  What is 4 x 6?

**684.** What is 3 x 4?

**685.** What is 5 x 5?

**686.** What is 9 x 5?

**687.** What is 8 divided by 4?

**688.** In the equation 8 divided by 4 equals 2, is the quotient 4 or 2?

**689.** What is 10 divided by 2?

**690.** What is 20 divided by 5?

**691.** What is 18 divided by 3? (Division facts 0-10)

**692.** If 8 divided by 2 equals 4, does 2 times 4 equal 8?

**693.** If 9 divided by 3 equals 3, does 3 times 3 equal 9? (Inverse operations)

**694.** Is a fraction part of a whole number?

**695.** Can a fraction also be written as a percentage?

**696.** Is the numerator the top number or the bottom number of a fraction?

**697.** Is the denominator the top number or the bottom number of a fraction?

**698.** How would you write the fraction one fourth?

**699.** How would you write the fraction one half?

**700.** How would you write the fraction one third?

**701.** Which fraction is greater: ½ or ¼?

**702.** Which set of fractions is ordered greatest to least: 6/9, 6/8, 6/7 or 6/7, 6/8, 6/9?

**703.** On which color is a spinner arrow most likely to land if ¾ of it is shaded red and ¼ is shaded blue?

**704.** Would fractions be important in reading a recipe?

**705.** What is the fraction of the pizza I ate if I ate 4 slices of a pizza that was divided into 8 pieces?

**706.** If you eat 2 pieces of a pie that is cut into 3 slices, how much have you eaten: ¾ or 2/3?

**707.** What is the fraction if 8 squares are shaded in on a shape having 12 squares: ¾ or 2/3?

**708.** What is the fraction if there are 10 triangles and five of them are shaded in?

**709.** Is 2/4 the same as ½?

**710.** If you look at a drawing where 6 out of 7 shapes are shaded yellow, and the other is shaded red, what fraction of the drawing is shaded red?

711. If you serve tomato soup into 2 bowls and chicken soup into one bowl, what is the fraction to indicate how many bowls are filled with the tomato soup?

712. What types of fractions and ingredients do you think might be part of a recipe for cookies?

713. If a number is 5 or greater, is that number rounded up or down?

714. What number can you round 14 to?

715. What number can you round 87 to?

716. What number can you round 26 to?

717. What number can you round 32 to?

718. What is 27 rounded to the nearest ten?

719. How do you round 76 to the nearest ten?

720. How do you round 165 to the nearest ten?

721. How do you round 7,558 to the nearest thousand?

722. What number am I if I have a one in the ones place, am greater than 65, but less than 81?

723. If the price of an ice cream cone is $2.99, what would you round it to?

724. If the temperature is 88 degrees, what would you round it to?

725. Can you tell time on an analog (face) clock to the minute?

726. What time is it now?

727. How many seconds are there in one minute?

728. How many minutes are there in one hour?

729. How many hours are there in one day?

730. How many days are there in one week?

731. How many weeks are there in one month?

732. How many months are there in one year?

733. How days are there in one year?

734. What is the average number of days in one month?

735. What is the missing time word: day, _, month, and year?

736. What is the missing time: 1:00, 1:30, _, 2:30?

737. What time is it if the big hand is on the 12 and the little hand on the 9?

**738.** What time would it say on a digital clock if it is a quarter to 3?

**739.** What would it say on a digital clock if it is half past 2?

**740.** What time would it on a digital clock if it is a quarter after 7?

**741.** What time would it show on a face clock if the digital clock read 8:45?

**742.** Do we change the clock time by one hour in spring and fall to preserve daylight?

**743.** Do different areas of the world live in different time zones?

**744.** Do you know the name of our time zone?

**745.** Do most people eat supper in the a.m. or the p.m?

**746.** What time of day do you eat breakfast: the a.m. or the p.m?

**747.** If the snowstorm started at 10:00 and it snowed for 4 hours, what time was it when it stopped?

**748.** How many hours is Amy at work each day if she arrives at 9 in the morning and leaves at 3 in the afternoon?

**749.** What is the temperature on a thermometer if the red mercury is halfway between the 30 and the 40?

**750.** What is your height?

**751.** What is your weight?

**752.** How many ounces are in one pound?

**753.** How many pounds are in one ton?

**754.** How many pounds are in one and one half tons?

**755.** Can you name something that weighs over one ton?

**756.** What is the metric unit for weight/mass: a gram or a kilometer?

**757.** Which is a better estimate for the weight of a football: 16 ounces or 16 pounds?

**758.** What is the better estimate for the weight of a frying pan: 2 kilograms or 2 grams?

**759.** Which is more: 3000 grams or 4 kilograms?

**760.** Can you estimate the height of your dresser?

**761.** Can you estimate the length of your dresser?

**762.** What is the metric unit for length: a meter or a foot?

**763.** Can you put these in order from smallest to largest: kilometer, centimeter, millimeter

**764.** How many inches are there in one foot?

**765.** How many feet are there in one yard?

**766.** Can you estimate in inches the length of your shoe?

**767.** Which is the better estimate for the length of a submarine sandwich: 12 feet or 12 inches?

**768.** If Joey's car is 9 feet long, and Luke's car is 2 feet longer than Joey's car, how long is Luke's car?

**769.** Which is the better estimate for the length of a hockey skate: 25 meters or 25 centimeters?

**770.** Can you estimate the distance in feet between your bed and the door?

**771.** What is the metric unit for distance: a gram or a kilometer?

**772.** Which distance is greater: one kilometer or one mile?

**773.** Can you estimate in miles the distance between your house and your school? (Etc.)

**774.** Can you put the following in order from smallest to largest: foot, yard, and inch?

**775.** Which is longer: a yard stick or a meter stick?

**776.** Can you put the following in order from smallest to largest: quart; gallon; pint; cup

**777.** What is the metric unit for volume: a liter or a quart?

**778.** Which is the better estimate for the volume of a coffee pot: 2 milliliters or 2 liters?

**779.** Which is more: 2000 milliliters or 1 liter?

**780.** Which is the better estimate for the volume of a mug of hot chocolate: 12 fluid ounces or 12 pints?

**781.** Which is more: 4 cups or 1 pint?

**782.** How many cups are equal to 1 pint?

**783.** Which liquid measurement would you use when following a recipe: cups or pints?

**784.** Which tool would you use to time a 40 yard dash: a yard stick or a stopwatch?

**785.** What would you use a thermometer to measure?

**786.** What would you use a yardstick to measure?

**787.** What would you use a scale to measure?

**788.** What would you use a tablespoon to measure?

**789.** What would you use a cup to measure?

**790.** What is the date today?

**791.** Which month comes before November?

**792.** Which month comes after June?

**793.** How many days does July have: 28, 30, or 31?

**794.** How many days does December have: 28, 30, or 31?

**795.** How many days does February have unless it is a leap year: 28, 30, or 31?

**796.** How many days does February have in a leap year: 28, 29, or 30?

**797.** What is the date tomorrow if today is August 31st?

**798.** What was the date yesterday if today is May 1st?

**799.** What is the date tomorrow if today is December 31st?

**800.** What other number changes on January 1st?

**801.** What is the year called when there are 29 days in February?

**802.** What day of the week is today?

**803.** What day was the day before yesterday?

**804.** If the party is a day after tomorrow and today is Wednesday, on which day is the party?

**805.** If tomorrow is Monday, what day was yesterday?

**806.** If yesterday was Friday, what day is tomorrow?

**807.** Is a calendar used to measure the time of year it is?

**808.** What are the 3 months of winter?

**809.** What are the 3 months of spring?

**810.** What are the 3 months of summer?

**811.** What are the 3 months of autumn?

**812.** What season comes before winter?

**813.** What season comes after spring?

**814.** Can you say the specific date of a holiday we celebrate?

**815.** Do addresses have numbers in them?

**816.** What is our house number?

**817.** What is our phone number?

**818.** Do we use both metal and paper for money?

**819.** Do different countries use different coins and paper or currency?

**820.** Can you name the currency of another country?

**821.** Do you think the Canadian dollar and Australian dollar have the same value as the American dollar?

**822.** Do you know the name of the currency in England that is named for its weight?

**823.** Which coin is worth 25 cents?

**824.** Which coin is worth 10 cents?

**825.** Which coin is worth 5 cents?

**826.** Which coin is worth 1 cent?

**827.** How many cents is one quarter worth?

**828.** How many quarters are in one dollar?

**829.** Does one quarter equal one fourth or one half of a dollar?

**830.** How many cents is one dime equal to?

**831.** How many cents is one nickel equal to?

**832.** How many dimes and nickels would equal one quarter?

**833.** What coin combinations can equal 25 cents besides one quarter?

**834.** What coin combination is equal to 3 quarters: 6 dimes and 3 nickels or 2 dimes and 10 nickels?

**835.** What is the difference in the equation: 25 cents minus 10 cents?

**836.** How many pennies are there in one dollar?

**837.** How many pennies are in one quarter?

**838.** How many nickels would equal one dime?

**839.** How many nickels would equal one quarter?

**840.** What would 25 cents and 15 cents add up to?

**841.** Is there a 50 cent coin?

**842.** What is a 50 cent piece equal to: one quarter or to one half dollar?

**843.** How many quarters equal 50 cents?

**844.** How many 50 cent pieces would equal one paper dollar?

**845.** How much money would you have if you have two quarters?

**846.** How much money would you have if you have one quarter, one dime, one nickel, and one penny?

**847.** How much money would you have if you have one quarter, one dime, and 3 pennies?

**848.** What much money do Tim and Lisa have together if Tim has 3 nickels and Lisa has 3 quarters?

849. What is equal on one quarter: 2 dimes and one nickel, or 1 dime and 4 nickels?

850. How can you make 30 cents with the least number of coins?

851. How can you make 46 cents with the least number of coins?

852. Do you have enough money to purchase a candy bar if you have one quarter and one nickel and it costs 40 cents?

853. Do you have enough money to purchase a box of colored pencils that costs 89 cents if you have three quarters, one dime, and one nickel?

854. If you have a dollar bill, two quarters, and two nickels do you have enough to buy a jumbo muffin that costs $1.65?

855. If you have two quarters and 3 dimes, how much more do you need to equal one dollar?

856. Did you receive the correct amount of change if you received 35 cents back from your dollar bill for a cereal bar that costs 65 cents?

857. If you buy a bottle of water that costs 75 cents, and you paid with one dollar, what would you receive back in change?

858. If a daily pass to the pool costs $4 and you paid with a ten dollar bill, what would your change be?

859. If you purchase a shirt that costs $15 and a pair of shoes that cost $30, what would your total be?

860. Do we have currency in denominations of one dollar, five dollars, ten dollars, twenty dollars, fifty dollars, and one hundred dollar bills?

861. What important historical people are pictured on our American coins and dollars?

862. If you are keeping track of how many blue cars you see on the way to the park, would you make tally marks?

863. After every four *tally marks* you make, how should you write the 5th tally mark?

864. Is the 5th tally mark in a tally a slash mark straight across or on a diagonal?

865. Would a line running east and west be horizontal or vertical?

866. Would a line running north and south be horizontal or vertical?

867. What would be a good way to show the population of our city from the last 10 years: tally marks or a bar graph?

868. Do you think that the bars on the graph would be higher or lower as the years progress?

869. Would a bar graph be a good way to show an increase or decrease in the data you have collected?

870. In which sport would the score typically be the highest: soccer, baseball, football, or basketball?

871. In which sport would the score typically be the lowest: soccer, football, or basketball?

872. Would circles, squares, triangles, rectangles be considered geometric shapes or organic shapes?

873. Can you name something in the environment that is round?

874. What can you name in the environment that is rectangular in shape?

875. What can you name in the environment that might be triangular?

876. What can you name in the environment that might be oval in shape?

877. What can you name that is in the shape of a sphere?

878. What can you name that is in the shape of a cone?

879. What object is in the shape of a cylinder?

880. Do we add or multiply the length of the sides together if we want to find the perimeter of a shape?

881. What is the perimeter of a 4-sided shape where each of the sides is 5 centimeters long?

882. What is the perimeter of a triangle if the sides measure 3 feet, 5 feet, and 7 feet?

883. What is the perimeter of a tree house if it measures 6 feet wide and 10 feet long: 16 feet or 32 feet?

884. Do you find the area of a square multiplying the base times itself or the base times two?

885. What is the area of a square with a side measuring 4 inches: 8 or 16?

886. What is the area of a square with a side measuring 3 inches: 12 or 9?

887. There are 5 red M & M's and 1 yellow M &M. If you reached for one without looking, how likely is it that you would pick the yellow one: certain, probable, unlikely, or impossible?

888. How do we find the range of a group of numbers: add the highest number with the lowest, or subtract the lowest number from the highest number?

889. What is the range in the sequence of numbers 5, **1**, 3, **10** and, 8?

890. What is the term for the value that appears most often in a sequence of numbers: mode or median?

891. What is the mode of 5, 8, 5, 6, 5, 7, 5, and 9?

## Math -- 3rd Grade

892. What do we call the number that has no value?

893. What do we call the highest number that suggests no end?

894. Can you count to 1000?

895. Can you skip-count to 1000 by hundreds?

896. Could Claire have been skip-counting by threes if she started at 32 and ended at 41?

897. How would you write the number ten??

898. How would you write the number fifty-six using digits?

899. How would you write the number four hundred fourteen using digits?

900. How would you write one hundred?

901. How would you write one thousand?

902. How would you write ten thousand?

903. How would you write one hundred thousand?

904. What number would come after 99?

905. What number would come after 999?

906. What number would come after 9,999?

907. What number would come after 99,999?

908. What is 2,999 + 1?

909. What is 54,099 + 1?

910. What is 234,999 +1?

911. What number would come before ten thousand?

912. What odd number comes after 55?

913. What is the even number that comes right after 178?

914. In the number 2,136, in which place is the 2: the hundreds or the thousands?

915. How many thousands, hundreds, and ones is the number 6,295 is equal to?

916. In which place is the number 7 in the number 7,528?

917. In which place is the number 5 in the number 7,528?

**918.** In which place is the number 2 in the number 7,528?

**919.** In which place is the number 8 in the number 7,528?

**920.** In the number 2,589, which digit is in the thousands place?

**921.** In the number 2,589, which digit is in the hundreds place?

**922.** In the number 2,589, which digit is in the tens place?

**923.** In the number 2,589, which digit is in the ones place?

**924.** Can you guess the two digit number that has a six in the tens place, and you say it when you count to 100 by tens?

**925.** How would you read the number *eight (comma) three two nine*?

**926.** How would you read the number four six (comma) eight one seven?

**927.** How would you read the number three *two eight (comma) five four two?*

**928.** How would you convert the place values of five thousand: it is equal to 50 tens or 500 tens?

**929.** How would you convert the place values of three thousand: it is equal to 30 hundreds or 300 hundreds?

**930.** What is 400 + 70 + 6 in its standard form?

**931.** What is 9, 325 in its expanded form: 9000+_?

**932.** How would you complete the pattern: 7+5=12, _+ 50=120, _+ 500=1,200, _+ 5,000=12,000?

**933.** Which number makes the equation true: 100 + 200 = 150 + _?

**934.** How can you balance the following equation: 250 +150 = 300 + _?

**935.** Can you add two numbers that each have three digits?

**936.** What is the sum of 222 and 111?

**937.** Is the difference in the equation 70 - 30 even or odd?

**938.** What number is missing in the sequence: 48, 38, 28, _?

**939.** On an input/output table, what is the rule if the input number reads 28 and the output number reads 38: add 10 or subtract 10?

**940.** How would you put the following numbers in order from least to greatest: 65, 35, and 55?

**941.** Is the number 736 greater than, less than, or equal to 636?

**942.** Is 18 + 4 greater than, less than, or equal to 16 + 5?

**943.** Is 78 + 3 greater than, less than, or equal to 75 + 6?

**944.** Is 45 + 5 greater than, less than, or equal to 25 + 26?

**945.** Can you add numbers that have 3 or more digits?

**946.** Can you subtract numbers that have 3 or more digits?

**947.** How can you balance the following equation: 300 -100 = 500 - _?

**948.** Which is the **equation**: 30+7=37 or 30 + 7?

**949.** When we round numbers, can we round to the nearest ten, hundred, thousand, or hundred thousand?

**950.** What is the rule when rounding numbers 5 or above: round up or round down?

**951.** What is the number 65 rounded to the nearest ten?

**952.** What is the number 32 rounded to the nearest ten?

**953.** What is 14 rounded to the nearest ten?

**954.** What is 97 rounded to the nearest ten?

**955.** What is 140 rounded to the nearest hundred?

**956.** What is 360 rounded to the nearest hundred?

**957.** What is 333 rounded to the nearest hundred?

**958.** What is 573 rounded to the nearest hundred?

**959.** What is 7,262 rounded to the nearest thousand?

**960.** What is 439,222 rounded to the nearest thousand?

**961.** What is 76,500 rounded to the nearest ten thousand?

**962.** What is 198,000 rounded to the nearest hundred thousand?

**963.** What is $8.25 rounded to the nearest dollar?

**964.** What is $49.99 rounded to the nearest dollar?

**965.** If you estimate the sum of 67 + 31, what would you round each number to and what would be the estimated sum?

**966.** If you estimate the difference of 49 – 22, what would you round each number to and what would be the estimated sum?

**967.** To help you subtract numbers mentally, is it helpful to round the number 49 to number 50?

**968.** How would you mentally subtract 49 - 18? (50-_ = _)

**969.** How would you mentally add 28 + 54? (30 + _=_)

**970.**  How would you estimate the product of 28 x 4?

**971.**  How would you estimate the quotient of 32 ÷ 3?

**972.**  Are the digits we are familiar with called Arabic numerals or Roman numerals?

**973.**  What are the numerals called that date back to the ancient Romans?

**974.**  What is Roman numeral I equal to?

**975.**  What is Roman numeral V equal to?

**976.**  What is Roman numeral X equal to?

**977.**  What is Roman numeral L equal to?

**978.**  What is Roman numeral C equal to?

**979.**  What is Roman numeral D equal to: 500 or 1,000?

**980.**  What is Roman numeral M equal to: 500 or 1,000?

**981.**  Do you place a Roman numeral that has the same value or the lesser value to the right or the left of that numeral?

**982.**  Do you place a Roman numeral that has the greater value to the right or left of another numeral?

**983.**  If you have "V" and then "I" together do you add or subtract their values?

**984.**  If you have "I" and then "V" together do you add or subtract their values?

**985.**  Is "I" and then "V" the same as 5 - 1 =4 or is it 1 + 5 =6?

**986.**  What is Roman numeral II?

**987.**  What is Roman numeral XV?

**988.**  What is Roman numeral XXX?

**989.**  What is Roman numeral IV?

**990.**  What is Roman numeral IX?

**991.**  What is Roman numeral XIV?

**992.**  What number is Super Bowl XXXVI?

**993.**  Are Roman numerals often used to show the date that a movie was made?

**994.**  What is the year MXMLXXX?

**995.**  What number would MD be if M equals 1,000 and D equals 500?

**996.**  How would you write 205 as a Roman numeral?

**997.** Can you say all the ordinal numbers first through tenth?

**998.** What is the date today using an ordinal number?

**999.** How would you say the king's name Louis "X", "I", "V" as an ordinal number?

**1000.** What ordinal is after 49<sup>th</sup>?

**1001.** Are there both positive and negative numbers in daily life?

**1002.** What kind of number is a surplus: a positive or a negative?

**1003.** What kind of number is a deficit: a positive or a negative?

**1004.** If the temperature is below zero, is that a positive or a negative number?

**1005.** If the number of people that are unemployed or not currently working is 8%, does that number represent a positive number or a negative number?

**1006.** If you owe me $5, is that a negative number or a positive number to you?

**1007.** If you have 300 pennies in your piggy bank, is that a positive number or a negative number?

**1008.** What is the fourth basic operation of arithmetic besides addition, subtraction, and multiplication?

**1009.** When we use the operation of multiplication, do we say two **times** or two **plus** three equals six?

**1010.** What letter is the symbol for multiplication?

**1011.** Is 3+3+3+3 the same as 4 **x** 3?

**1012.** Is 3x4 the same as 4x3?

**1013.** In the equation $2 \times 3 = 6$, are the numbers *two* and *three* the factors or the product?

**1014.** In the equation $5 \times 5 = 25$, which number is the product?

**1015.** Is the equation 9 x 7 (nine times seven) the same as 7 x 9?

**1016.** Can the equation 9 x 7 also be written vertically or up and down?

**1017.** What is the name of the table we can use to find the product of all combinations of factors?

**1018.** What is the product of 0 x 0? (1x0, 2x0, 3x0, 4x0, 5x0, 6x0, 7x0, 8x0, 9x0)

**1019.** What is the product of 1 x 1? (1x2, 1x3, 1x4, 1x5, 1x6, 1x7, 1x8, 1x9)

**1020.** What is the product of 2 x 1? (2x2, 2x3, 2x4, 2x5, 2x6, 2x7, 2x8, 2x9)

**1021.** What is the product of 3 x 1? (3x2, 3x3, 3x4, 3x5, 3x6, 3x7, 3x8, 3x9)

**1022.** What is the product of 4 x 1? (4x2, 4x3, 4x4, 4x5, 4x6, 4x7, 4x8, 4x9)

**1023.** What is the product of 5 x 1? (5x2, 5x3, 5x4, 5x5, 5x6, 5x7, 5x8, 5x9)

**1024.** What is the product of 6 x 1? (6x2, 6x3, 6x4, 6x5, 6x6, 6x7, 6x8, 6x9)

**1025.** What is the product of 7 x 1? (7x2, 7x3, 7x4, 7x5, 7x6, 7x7, 7x8, 7x9)

**1026.** What is the product of 8 x 1? (8x2, 8x3, 8x4, 8x5, 8x6, 8x7, 8x8, 8x9)

**1027.** What is the product of 9 x 1? (9x2, 9x3, 9x4, 9x5, 9x6, 9x7, 9x8, 9x9)

**1028.** What is the product of 10 x 1? (10x2, 10x3, 10x4, 10x5, 10x6, 10x7, 10x8, 10x9)

**1029.** If you are solving for "s" and s x 4 = 20, then s = ___?

**1030.** What is the product of 20 x 5?

**1031.** What is the product of 200 x 5?

**1032.** In computing 200 x 5, you would multiply 2 x 5 and then add how many zeros?

**1033.** If Adam bought 3 sets of dominos and each set had 200 pieces, how many dominos does Adam have in all?

**1034.** What is the product of 2,000 x 5?

**1035.** What is 333 x 2?

**1036.** What is the product of 2 x 3 x 5?

**1037.** If part of an equation is set off in parenthesis, would you compute that operation first or second?

**1038.** What is the name of the math property whereby multiplying a number by a group of numbers added together and set off in parenthesis is the same as doing each multiplication operation separately as in 3 x (2 + 4) is equal to 3x2 + 3x4, which is the same as 3 x 6: commutative or distributive?

**1039.** In the equation 10(3+2) = *a*, and the 3 + 2 is in parenthesis, what would *a* equal?

**1040.** Using the distributive property, what is two times (three plus four) equal to? 2(3+4)

**1041.** What is the name of the name of the algebra property whereby you can multiply and add and it does not matter how you group the numbers: the associative or the distributive?

**1042.** Using the associative property of re-grouping, what is 2(3x4) (*Two times three times four in parenthesis*) equal to: (2x3) times _?

**1043.** What is the name of the math property where changing the order of the numbers does not change the result: the commutative property or the distributive property?

**1044.** Using the commutative property, what is 2x3 equal to?

**1045.** What is the name of the math property of addition and multiplication whereby if you add any number to 0, the sum will be that number, and if you multiply any number by 1, the product will be that number: the identity property or the commutative property?

**1046.** In the identity property of addition, 22 plus **what** equals 22? (22 + _ = 22)

**1047.** In the identity property of multiplication, 6 times **what** equals 6? (6 x _ = 6)

**1048.** Is 1x8 = 8 an example of the identity, distributive, associative, or the commutative property of multiplication?

**1049.** What is the name of the math property of multiplication where it follows that 2(3x4) (*Two times, three times four in parenthesis*) equals (2x3)4 (*Two times three in parenthesis, times four*): identity, associative, or commutative?

**1050.** Is 2x4=4x2 an example of the associative or the commutative property of multiplication?

**1051.** Is 2(3+1) (*Two times, three plus one in parenthesis*) = 2 x 3 + 2 x 1 an example of the identity, distributive, associative, or the commutative property of multiplication?

**1052.** What is the name of the number that is the product of an integer times itself: a square number or a quotient?

**1053.** Can multiplication problems be represented as square numbers?

**1054.** In the equation 3 x 3 = 9, which number is the *square* number?

**1055.** Are the numbers 16 and 25 also square numbers?

**1056.** What is the product or perfect square of 5x5?

**1057.** What is the product or perfect square of 4x4?

**1058.** What is the product or perfect square of 7x7?

**1059.** What is the product or perfect square of 10x10?

**1060.** If 3 multiplied by itself is 9, is the number 3 the *square root* of 9?

**1061.** What is the square root of 25?

**1062.** What is the square root of 16?

**1063.** What is the square root of 49?

**1064.** What is the square root of 100?

**1065.** What number is 6 the square root of?

**1066.** Can you multiply two and three numbers together?

**1067.** What is another way of writing 786? (7 x__ =700), + (8 x___ = ___), + ___

**1068.** If Lucas scored 8 points in the basketball game, and Jonathon scored 3 times as many points as Lucas, how many points did Jonathon score?

**1069.** If the *inverse* operation of addition is subtraction, what is the inverse operation of multiplication?

**1070.** How many groups of 6 are there in 18?

**1071.** If there are 3 groups of 6 in 18, then what can we say eighteen divided by six is equal to?

**1072.** What does a division symbol look like?

**1073.** In the equation 6 divided by 3 = 2, what is the quotient: the number 2 or the number 3?

**1074.** In the equation 6 divided by 3 = 2, is the number 6 the dividend or the divisor?

**1075.** In the equation 6 divided by 3 = 2, is the number 3 the dividend or the divisor?

**1076.** What is 0 divided by any number?

**1077.** What is the quotient of any number divided by 1, like $7 \div 1$?

**1078.** What is the quotient of $2 \div 2$? ($4 \div 2$, $6 \div 2$, $8 \div 2$, $10 \div 2$, $12 \div 2$, $14 \div 2$, $16 \div 2$, $18 \div 2$, $20 \div 2$)?

**1079.** What is the quotient of $3 \div 3$? ($6 \div 3$, $9 \div 3$, $12 \div 3$, $15 \div 3$, $18 \div 3$, $21 \div 3$, $24 \div 3$, $27 \div 3$, $30 \div 3$)?

**1080.** What is the quotient of $4 \div 4$? ($8 \div 4$, $12 \div 4$, $16 \div 4$, $20 \div 4$, $24 \div 4$, $28 \div 4$, $32 \div 4$, $36 \div 4$, $40 \div 4$)?

**1081.** What is the quotient of $5 \div 5$? ($10 \div 5$, $15 \div 5$, $20 \div 5$, $25 \div 5$, $30 \div 5$, $35 \div 5$, $40 \div 5$, $45 \div 5$, $50 \div 5$)?

**1082.** What is the quotient of $6 \div 6$? ($12 \div 6$, $18 \div 6$, $24 \div 6$, $30 \div 6$, $36 \div 6$, $42 \div 6$, $48 \div 6$, $54 \div 6$, $60 \div 6$)?

**1083.** What is the quotient of $7 \div 7$? ($14 \div 7$, $21 \div 7$, $28 \div 7$, $35 \div 7$, $42 \div 7$, $49 \div 7$, $56 \div 7$, $63 \div 7$, $70 \div 7$)?

**1084.** What is the quotient of $8 \div 8$? ($16 \div 8$, $24 \div 8$, $32 \div 8$, $40 \div 8$, $48 \div 8$, $56 \div 8$, $64 \div 8$, $72 \div 8$, $80 \div 8$)?

**1085.** What is the quotient of $9 \div 9$? ($18 \div 9$, $27 \div 9$, $36 \div 9$, $45 \div 9$, $54 \div 9$, $63 \div 9$, $72 \div 9$, $81 \div 9$, $90 \div 9$)?

**1086.** What is the quotient of $10 \div 10$? ($20 \div 10$, $30 \div 10$, $40 \div 10$, $50 \div 10$, $60 \div 10$, $70 \div 10$, $80 \div 10$, $90 \div 10$, $100 \div 10$)?

**1087.** What is the quotient of $11 \div 11$? ($22 \div 11$, $33 \div 11$, $44 \div 11$, $55 \div 11$, $66 \div 11$, $77 \div 11$, $88 \div 11$, $99 \div 11$, $110 \div 11$)?

**1088.** What is the quotient of $12 \div 12$? ($24 \div 12$, $36 \div 12$, $48 \div 12$, $60 \div 12$, $72 \div 12$, $84 \div 12$, $96 \div 12$, $108 \div 12$, $120 \div 12$)?

**1089.** If Kristin has 3 dozen or 36 daisies, and she wants to divide them equally into 6 vases, how many daisies would she put in each vase?

**1090.** Is the following an example of an inverse or a reverse operation: $1 + 4 = 5$, so $5 - 4 = 1$?

**1091.** What is the inverse of $42 \div 7 = 6$? ($6 \times 7 =$ ___)

**1092.** Which of the following equations is equal to $3 \times 4$: $3+3+3+3$, or $4+4+4+4$?

**1093.** What is the inverse of $20-5=15$? ($15+$ ___ $=$ ___)

**1094.** What is the related multiplication fact for 12÷6=2?

**1095.** What is 100 ÷2?

**1096.** What is 700 ÷ 7?

**1097.** What is 210 ÷3?

**1098.** What is 320 ÷4?

**1099.** What is 280 ÷7?

**1100.** What is 810 ÷9?

**1101.** Is 2,420 divisible by 2?

**1102.** Is 2,425 divisible by 2?

**1103.** Is 250 divisible by 5?

**1104.** Is 256 divisible by 5?

**1105.** Is 240 divisible by 10?

**1106.** Is 223 divisible by 10?

**1107.** What is the math term for the amount left over after a division computation: the dividend or the remainder?

**1108.** In the equation 22÷7, 7 does not go into 22 evenly so would we have a *remainder*?

**1109.** In the equation 9÷4, what would the remainder be? (4x2=8 R __)

**1110.** In the equation 30÷4, what would the quotient and the remainder be?

**1111.** What is the name for the table that shows output values for a number of different inputs?

**1112.** What is the rule on an input/output table if one input number is 8 and its output number is 4, and another input number is 10 and its output number is 5?

**1113.** Is the inverse of 7 x 6=42 the division operation 42 ÷6=7?

**1114.** To finish the equation, __÷5 = 4, would you multiply or add 5 and 4?

**1115.** How would you finish the equation: __÷4 = 3?

**1116.** When you have a math equation with a letter, is that letter called the **variable** or the **integer?**

**1117.** What is the *variable* in the equation b÷2 = 6?

**1118.** What is the answer to this equation: b÷2=6?

**1119.** Can variables be used for all operations: addition, subtraction, multiplication, and division?

**1120.** What is the division equation for ½ of 28?

**1121.** Can you finish the following division pattern: 5÷5=__, 50÷5=__, 500÷5=__, 5000÷5=__?

**1122.** Solve the following word problem: Jack and his mom want to buy 24 cupcakes for Jack's birthday treat for his class. If there are 8 cupcakes in each package, how many packages of cupcakes do Jack and his mom need to buy?

**1123.** How would you write the division equation for 24 cupcakes, 3 packages, and 8 cupcakes in each package?

**1124.** What are numbers that are parts of a whole called: fractions or decimals?

**1125.** What are two other common fractions besides ½?

**1126.** What is the top number of a fraction called?

**1127.** What is the bottom number of a fraction called?

**1128.** Does the bottom number of a fraction or denominator tell how many parts the whole is divided into?

**1129.** If the numerator and the denominator are the same, what whole number does that fraction equal?

**1130.** Are 0, 1, 2, 3, 4 whole numbers or fractions?

**1131.** Is 13/4 a whole number or a mixed number?

**1132.** What two numbers is 1 ½ between?

**1133.** What is the denominator in the fraction 2/3?

**1134.** What is the numerator in the fraction ¾?

**1135.** Are measurements often indicated with fractions like 5 ¼ inches?

**1136.** What is the numerator indicating that the two fractions are equal: 2/3 = __/9?

**1137.** Can fractions be reduced to their lowest terms?

**1138.** What is the lowest term of 2/4?

**1139.** What can 5/10 be reduced to?

**1140.** What can 6/8 be reduced to?

**1141.** What is the equivalent fraction of 3/6: ½ or 2/3?

**1142.** Can you add and subtract fractions?

**1143.** What is the sum of ½ + ½?

**1144.** What is the sum of ¼ + 2/4?

**1145.** What is the difference of 7/8 – 4/8?

**1146.** Is 5/8 greater than, less than, or equal to 3/8?

**1147.** If a square is divided into 8 equal parts and 5 of those parts are shaded in, what is the fraction of the area that is shaded?

**1148.** If a pizza is sliced into 8 slices and there are 2 slices left after everyone takes a piece, how much of the pizza was eaten?

**1149.** If you wanted to find ¼ of 20 would you divide or multiply 20 by 4?

**1150.** What is division equation for 1/3 of 18? (18÷__ = __)

**1151.** Can a fraction be represented with a decimal point?

**1152.** What is the number 2 and 4/10 equal to, using a decimal? (2.__)

**1153.** What is .25 as a fraction?

**1154.** What is .50 as a fraction?

**1155.** What is .75 as a fraction?

**1156.** Can we show the hundredths' place by writing 1/100 = .01?

**1157.** What is .08 as a fraction: 8/10 or 8/100?

**1158.** What would 8/100 be reduced to in lowest terms: 4/50 or 2/25?

**1159.** What is .6 as a fraction: 2/3 or ¾?

**1160.** What is 9 and 81/100 as a decimal number?

**1161.** What is four and three tenths as a decimal number: 4.03 or 4.30?

**1162.** What numbers are missing in the following pattern: 3.2, 3.3, 3._, 3._, 3.__?

**1163.** What is the sum of 2.5 and 3.1? (2+3 = __ / 5+1=__)

**1164.** What is the difference in 5.5 and 4.3? (5-4=__ / 5-3=__)

**1165.** What is the sum of 1.2 + 1.2 + 1.2?

**1166.** What is ¼ as a decimal?

**1167.** What is ¾ as a decimal?

**1168.** What is ½ as a decimal?

**1169.** Can you create and interpret bar graphs?

**1170.** Can you find coordinates on a graph?

**1171.** Can you graph points on a graph?

1172. Can you create and interpret line graphs?

1173. Can you create and interpret pictographs?

1174. Can you create and interpret a Venn diagram?

1175. In what location are the common characteristics located on a Venn diagram?

1176. How much money do you have in your (piggy) bank?

1177. What denominations of dollars are the most common?

1178. What is another name for money?

1179. Do different countries have different currencies?

1180. Does all money in all countries have the same value?

1181. What are all the coins we use and how much is each worth?

1182. How much would you have if you had one ten, two fives and three one dollar bills?

1183. How much would you have if you had two quarters, three dimes, one nickel, and four pennies?

1184. If you buy a box of cookies that costs $3.50, and you pay with a ten dollar bill, how much change would you get back?

1185. If a book you want to buy at the book fair costs $4.99 and you have four one dollar bills, three quarters, and two dimes, would you have enough money to buy the book?

1186. At the restaurant James ordered a hamburger for $4.00, Cristina ordered a chicken sandwich for $5.00, and Matthew ordered a roast beef sandwich for $7.00. What was the amount of the total bill before tax and tip?

1187. After a nice meal at a restaurant, Avery and her two friends receive a bill totaling $21.75. If they want to divide the total evenly among the three, how much would each person pay?

1188. If Katie wanted to buy 4 balloons and each balloon costs $2.00 each, how much would she pay in all?

1189. What instrument measures the temperature?

1190. What is the metric term for measuring temperature?

1191. What is the U.S. Customary term for measuring temperature?

1192. What is the temperature if the mercury is halfway between 40 and 50?

1193. What is 0 degrees Celsius equal to in degrees Fahrenheit: 32 or 98?

1194. What liquid can melt at thirty-two degrees Fahrenheit?

1195. If it is 85 degrees Fahrenheit, would the weather be hot or cold?

1196. If it is ten degrees below zero, would be weather be hot or cold?

1197. In the U.S. Customary System, what unit do we use to measure driving distance?

1198. Are there 5,280 feet in one mile or two miles?

1199. In the U.S. Customary System, what unit do we use to measure the length of a football field?

1200. In the U.S. Customary System, what unit do we use to measure the length of a 12 inch sub sandwich?

1201. How many inches is equal to one foot?

1202. How many feet are in one yard?

1203. How many inches are equal to one yard?

1204. In the U.S. Customary System what unit do we use to measure the length of a piece of wood?

1205. What kind of tools can you use make linear measurements?

1206. Can you estimate the length of an object without using any tools?

1207. In the U.S. Customary System, what unit do we use to weigh objects?

1208. What is the abbreviation of pound?

1209. What is the abbreviation of ounce?

1210. How many ounces are in one pound: 16 or 24?

1211. Does one pint equal 16 ounces?

1212. In the U.S. Customary System, what unit do we use for capacity, smallest to largest: pint, quart, cup, and gallon?

1213. How many cups are there in one pint?

1214. How many pints are there in one quart: ½ or 2?

1215. How many quarts are there in one gallon?

1216. What is the better estimate for the capacity of a can of paint: one pint or one gallon?

1217. If 2 pints equal 1 quart, and 4 quarts equal one gallon, how many pints equal one gallon?

1218. Which is more: 10 pints or one gallon?

1219. What are the Metric System units of length in order from smallest to largest: meter, centimeter, kilometer, and millimeter?

1220. What is the Metric system unit of weight: grams or pounds?

1221. Which is higher: one gram or one kilogram?

**1222.** What is one kilogram equal to: 1,000 grams or 2,000 grams?

**1223.** If the side of the balance with a ball is lower than the side of the balance with an apple, what can you conclude?

**1224.** What is the Metric System unit for liquid volume: the quart or the liter?

**1225.** What time is it?

**1226.** How many seconds are there in one minute?

**1227.** How many minutes are there in one hour?

**1228.** How many minutes are there in 3 hours?

**1229.** How many hours are there in one day?

**1230.** What is the abbreviation for the Latin phrase "**ante** meridiem" which means before noon?

**1231.** What is the abbreviation for the Latin phrase "**post** meridiem" which means after noon?

**1232.** What time is it if the little hand is on the eight and the big hand is on the nine?

**1233.** What time is it if the little hand is on the three and the big hand is on the eight?

**1234.** What time is it if the little hand is on the four and the big hand is on the four?

**1235.** What time is it if the little hand is on the seven and the big hand is on the eleven?

**1236.** What is another way of saying it is twelve o'clock in the middle of the day?

**1237.** What is another way of saying it is twelve o'clock in the middle of the night?

**1238.** What is another way of saying it is 3:40?

**1239.** What are the clock hands on if it is 2:35?

**1240.** If it is 4:30, what time will it be in 45 minutes?

**1241.** If the class went outside for a short recess at 10:20 a.m. and returned to the classroom at 10:45 a.m., how long was the recess?

**1242.** Can you read a time schedule?

**1243.** Can you read a timeline?

**1244.** What kinds of events are often sequenced on a timeline?

**1245.** What is the date today?

**1246.** If today is Thursday March 2nd, what is the day on Saturday?

**1247.** If today is Thursday August 2nd, what was the date on Tuesday?

**1248.** How can you say the date for today using only numbers? (__/__/__)

**1249.** How can you say the date of your birthday using only numbers?

**1250.** What day of the week is it today?

**1251.** What day of the week does our calendar begin with?

**1252.** How many days are there in one week?

**1253.** How many weeks are there in one month?

**1254.** How many days are there in one calendar year?

**1255.** What is the shortest month of the year?

**1256.** How often are there 29 days in the month of February?

**1257.** How many years are in one decade?

**1258.** How many years are in one century?

**1259.** How many years is one millennia equal to?

**1260.** What is the study of lines, point, shapes and angles called?

**1261.** What saying related to geometry describes what an acorn says when it grows up?

**1262.** Is a square a geometric shape?

**1263.** What geometric shapes can you name?

**1264.** What are flat, closed figures called having three or more straight lines: polygons or hexagons?

**1265.** Is a circle a polygon?

**1266.** Is a diamond shape a polygon?

**1267.** How are polygons formed: by line segments or by angle segments?

**1268.** What is a line called that runs left to right or east to west: horizontal or vertical?

**1269.** What is a line called that runs up and down or north and south: horizontal or vertical?

**1270.** What are two line segments called that cross through each other like the letter X: parallel or perpendicular?

**1271.** What are two line segments called that stay the same distance from each other and never cross: parallel or perpendicular?

**1272.** How many equal sides does a square have?

**1273.** What can you name that is square?

1274. How many sides does a rectangle have?

1275. What can you name that is rectangle?

1276. Are polygons shapes that have many angles?

1277. How many sides does a triangle have?

1278. What can you name that is in the shape of a triangle?

1279. If a triangle has three equal angles measuring 45 degrees each, is it an equilateral or isosceles triangle?

1280. What is the name of a triangle that has two equal sides, the angles measure less than 90 degrees, and the angles opposite the equal sides are also equal: equilateral or isosceles?

1281. How many sides (or edges) does a quadrilateral have?

1282. How many sides does a pentagon have?

1283. How many straight sides does a hexagon have?

1284. How many sides does a heptagon have?

1285. How many sides does an octagon have?

1286. What is a stop sign the shape of: a hexagon or an octagon?

1287. What is a straight line called with no points at either end: a line or a line segment?

1288. What is a straight line called with two points at either end: a ray or a line segment?

1289. What is a straight line called with a point at one end and an arrow at the other: a line or a ray?

1290. What is the point called in which two line segments meet: a corner or a vertex?

1291. How are vertices named: with letters or numbers?

1292. On a four-sided polygon, could you name the figure either ABCD, DCBA, or both?

1293. Are the vertices like the points of the shape?

1294. What property does a closed shape have besides vertices: angles or rays?

1295. When two sides of a polygon meet, what does it form?

1296. What is an angle called that forms a square corner: a right angle or a left angle?

1297. How many right angles do rectangles and squares have?

1298. What are shapes called the have exactly the same size and shape: symmetrical or congruent?

1299. When a shape or figure can be folded in half and both halves match up, is the figure symmetrical or congruent?

**1300.** What is the name of the fold line when a shape is folded in half: the dividing line or the line of symmetry?

**1301.** How many lines of symmetry does a square have?

**1302.** How many lines of symmetry does a circle have?

**1303.** Can shapes be similar but not congruent?

**1304.** If a shape like the letter "P" is flipped over and reversed onto another grid, how has this shape been transformed: reflected, rotated, or translated?

**1305.** If a shape like the letter "P" stays the same but is shifted slightly to the right on another grid, how has this shape been transformed: reflected, rotated, or translated?

**1306.** If a shape like the letter "P" turns over on its side on another grid, how has this shape been transformed: reflected, rotated, or translated?

**1307.** What is the distance around a shaped called: diameter or perimeter?

**1308.** In order to find the perimeter around a shape, do we *multiply* or *add* the lengths of all the sides together?

**1309.** If a rectangle has one line segment 4 inches long, and one line segment 3 inches long, what is the distance around or the perimeter of this rectangle?

**1310.** If a triangle has one line segment that is 3 centimeters long, one line segment that is 4 centimeters long, and a third line segment that is 2 centimeters long, what is its perimeter?

**1311.** What is the perimeter of a square that shows one side measuring 5 centimeters long?

**1312.** What is the perimeter of a rectangle that shows the long side measuring 6 centimeters long and the shorter side measuring 3 centimeters long?

**1313.** What is the value of the third side of a triangle if its total perimeter is 18 inches and one side measures 9 inches and the other side measures 5 inches?

**1314.** What is the number of square units called that cover a surface: its perimeter or its area?

**1315.** If a rectangle has an area of 8 square inches, would you write that as 8 inches square?

**1316.** To find the area of a shape do we multiply or divide the length of its sides?

**1317.** What is the area of a rectangle with one side measuring 6 inches long and the other side measuring 3 inches long?

**1318.** What is the area of a square with each side measuring 5 millimeters long?

**1319.** What are three-dimensional shapes called: shapes or solids?

**1320.** What are cylinders, pyramids, spheres, and prisms considered: shapes or solids?

**1321.** What is the bottom part of a pyramid called: its base or its surface?

**1322.** Which three-dimensional shape has both curved surfaces and flat surfaces: a pyramid or a sphere?

**1323.** Is the flat surface of a solid called a front or a face?

**1324.** Is the line segment where two faces meet on a prism: an edge or a vertex?

**1325.** Do the edges come together at the face or the vertex?

**1326.** Is the point of a cone called a vertex or a face?

**1327.** To find the volume of a three-dimension object like a cube, do we multiply or add the base, the side, and the height?

**1328.** What is the volume of a cube that has 5 square units on its face, 2 square units on its side, and 4 square units for its height? ___cubic units.

**1329.** What is your favorite area of math?

**1330.** How do we use math concepts in our everyday lives?

## Math – 4<sup>th</sup> Grade

**1331.** What place value comes after the ones?

**1332.** How many zeros are in the number 10?

**1333.** What place value comes after the tens?

**1334.** How many zeros are in the number 100?

**1335.** What place value comes after one hundred?

**1336.** How many zeros are in the number 1,000?

**1337.** What place value comes after one thousand?

**1338.** How many zeros are in the number 10,000?

**1339.** What place value comes after ten thousand?

**1340.** How many zeros are in the number 100,000?

**1341.** What place value comes after one hundred thousand?

**1342.** How many zeros are there in 1,000,000?

**1343.** What place value comes after one million?

**1344.** What place value comes after ten million?

**1345.** What place value comes after one hundred million?

**1346.** What is the next highest number place value after one thousand billion: one trillion or one quadrillion?

**1347.** What can you name that can be measured in the billions?

**1348.** If we write numbers larger than ten thousand, what do we have to write to show the correct place value?

**1349.** Moving right to left, how many digits do you count before inserting a comma?

**1350.** How would you read the number: one comma, two three four comma, five six seven?

**1351.** Do you *have to* use a comma for a number between one thousand and nine thousand nine hundred and ninety-nine?

**1352.** Is "three comma one two three" the same as "three one two three" with no comma?

**1353.** How many zeros are there in 1000?

**1354.** How many zeros are there in 100,000

**1355.** How many zeros are there in one million?

**1356.** How many zeros are there in 10,000?

**1357.** In the decimal system, what number are the place values based on?

**1358.** What do we call the time span of ten years?

**1359.** What do we call the time span of 100 years?

**1360.** How is the number "one hundred thousand five hundred" written in standard form?

**1361.** How is 8, 243 written in expanded form?

**1362.** Using digits how would you write the number five thousand, forty?

**1363.** Are numbers to the right of 0 on a number line positive or negative numbers?

**1364.** Are numbers to the left of 0 on a number line positive or negative numbers?

**1365.** Is 75-15 an odd or even number?

**1366.** Is the difference of 50-9 an odd or even number?

**1367.** Are negative numbers similar to having debt, or being in the "red?"

**1368.** Are positive number similar to showing a profit, or being in the "black?"

**1369.** Are the numerals zero through nine considered Arabic or Roman?

**1370.** Can you write the letters of the Roman numerals one through five?

**1371.** Can you write the letters of the Roman numerals six through ten?

**1372.** What Arabic number is the letter L equal to: 50 or 100?

**1373.** What Arabic number is the letter C equal to: 100 or 1,000?

**1374.** What Arabic number is the letter D equal to: 500 or 1,000?

**1375.** What Arabic number is the letter M equal to: 10,000 or 1,000?

**1376.** If smaller Roman numerals are on the left of a larger number, do we add or subtract that value?

**1377.** What is XL as an Arabic number?

**1378.** If smaller Roman numerals are on the right of a larger number, do we add or subtract that value?

**1379.** What is LX as an Arabic number?

**1380.** In Roman numerals if M=1000 and C=100 and L=50, what is MCL equal to?

**1381.** What is Roman numeral XVIII equal to?

**1382.** How would you write the year 2015 as a Roman numeral?

1383. Do some clocks have Roman numerals?

1384. What is the rule for rounding a number if it is four or less: round up or down to the nearest ten?

1385. What is the rule for rounding a number if it is five or more: round up or down to the nearest ten?

1386. What is 2,500 rounded to the nearest thousand?

1387. What is 2,200 rounded to the nearest thousand?

1388. What is 2,890 rounded to the nearest hundred?

1389. What is 2,255 rounded to the nearest ten?

1390. What is the name of a number that can only be divided by itself and by the number one: a prime number or a composite number?

1391. What is the name of a number that can be divided by at least one other number: a prime number or a composite number?

1392. If a number has only two factors, is it called a prime number or a composite number?

1393. Are zero and one prime numbers?

1394. What kind of numbers are 2, 3, 5, 7, 11, 13, and 17: prime numbers or composite numbers?

1395. What kind of numbers are 1, 2, 3, 6, 9, and 12: prime numbers or composite numbers?

1396. Is 28 a prime or composite number?

1397. Is 59 a prime or composite number?

1398. Can you add numbers up to one million?

1399. What does 50,000 and 90,000 equal?

1400. What does nine hundred thousand and one hundred thousand equal?

1401. What is the sum of six thousand, plus three hundred, plus fifty- two?

1402. What addition property is 1 + (2 + 3) in parenthesis = (1 + 2) in parenthesis + 3 an example of: the distributive or the associative?

1403. What addition property is 1 + 2= 2 + 1 an example of: the identity or the commutative?

1404. What addition property is 1 + 0 =1 an example of: the identity, distributive, or the associative?

1405. What is the approximate sum if you round to the nearest thousand and then add the following numbers together: 4,100 + 3,987?

1406. Can you subtract numbers up to one million?

1407. Do you not how to borrow from the higher place value when subtracting numbers?

**1408.** What is 185,000 – 84,000?

**1409.** What is 180,000 – 15,000?

**1410.** What is 1,000,000 – 650,000?

**1411.** Can you estimate the difference of 780 - 314?

**1412.** Do you know your multiplication facts up to the number up to 10 x 10?

**1413.** In the equation 3 x 8 = 24, which numbers are the factors?

**1414.** In the equation 2 x 8 = 24, which number is the product?

**1415.** What are some multiples of the number 2?

**1416.** What are some multiples of the number 6?

**1417.** What is the number 28 a multiple of?

**1418.** What is the number 81 a multiple of?

**1419.** What *two* numbers is 18 a multiple of?

**1420.** Is the number 96 a multiple of 12 or 14?

**1421.** What is it called when you take a number and multiply it by itself: a square or a multiplier?

**1422.** Is 4 x 4 = 16 the same is saying 4 squared equals 16?

**1423.** What is 2 x 2?

**1424.** What is 5 x 5?

**1425.** What is 6 x 6?

**1426.** What is 7 x 7?

**1427.** What is 8 x 8?

**1428.** What is 9 x 9?

**1429.** What is 10 x 10?

**1430.** What is the square root of 4?

**1431.** What is the square root of 36, or what number when multiplied by itself equals 36?

**1432.** What is the square root of 25?

**1433.** What is the square root of 81?

**1434.** What is the square root of 49?

**1435.** What is the square root of 121?

**1436.** What is the square root of 64?

**1437.** What is the square root of 144?

**1438.** What is the product of 3 x 4 x 2?

**1439.** When you are multiplying numbers by ten, what number do you add to the number that you are multiplying by: 0 or 1?

**1440.** What is the product of 44 x 10?

**1441.** What is the product of 220 x 10?

**1442.** Can you multiply by tens, hundreds, and thousands?

**1443.** What is a little trick you can use when you multiple numbers ending in zeros like 200 x 400?

**1444.** How many zeros would you add to find the product of 200 x 400?

**1445.** What is the product of 200 x 400: 8,000 or 80,000?

**1446.** What property is 1 x 5 = 5 an example of: the associative, distributive, identity, or zero property of multiplication?

**1447.** What property is 3 x (4-3) in parenthesis = 3 x 4 – 3 x 3 an example of: the associative, distributive, identity, or zero property of multiplication?

**1448.** What property is (1 x 3) in parenthesis x 4 = 1 x (3 x 4) in parenthesis an example of: the associative, distributive, identity, or zero property of multiplication?

**1449.** What property is 28 x 0 an example of: the associative, distributive, identity, or zero property of multiplication?

**1450.** What property is 22 x 1 and example of: the associative, distributive, identity or zero property of multiplication?

**1451.** How would you estimate the product of 4 x 3,120 rounding to the nearest thousand?

**1452.** What is the product of 7000 x 10 using the trick with adding the zeros?

**1453.** Is 2 x 8 greater than, less than, or equal to 15?

**1454.** Is 2 x 9 greater than, less than, or equal to 18?

**1455.** Is 5 x 8 greater than, less than, or equal to 45?

**1456.** What is the inverse operation of multiplication: division or addition?

**1457.** How would you invert the equation 10 x 2 = 20?

**1458.** How would you invert the equation 24 ÷ 8 = 3?

**1459.** What number is the *dividend* in the equation: 20 ÷ 5 = 4?

**1460.** What number is the *divisor* in the equation: $20 \div 5 = 4$?

**1461.** What number is the *quotient* in the equation: $20 \div 5 = 4$?

**1462.** What is the quotient of the problem: $72 \div 8$?

**1463.** In the equation $12 \div 3 = 4$, what does number 12 represent: the divisor or the dividend?

**1464.** In the equation $12 \div 3 = 4$, what does number 4 represent: the quotient or the divisor?

**1465.** In the equation $12 \div 3 = 4$, what does the number 3 represent: the divisor or the dividend?

**1466.** In the equation $20 \div 1 = 20$, what number is both the quotient and the dividend?

**1467.** Do you remember your division facts up to 12?

**1468.** What is any number divided by 1 equal to?

**1469.** What is the product of an equation where a number is divided by itself?

**1470.** How would you write $12 \div 3$ as a fraction?

**1471.** If there are 16 people in line for the rollercoaster and each car holds four people, how many cars will they fill up?

**1472.** What is a number called that divides another number evenly and does not have a remainder: a factor or a prime number?

**1473.** If $4 \div 4 = 1$, $4 \div 2 = 2$, and $4 \div 1 = 1$, what are the *factors* of 4?

**1474.** What are the factors of 24?

**1475.** What common factors do the numbers 20 and 24 have?

**1476.** If Brandon has 7 cookies and he wants to divide them equally among 3 lunch boxes, how many would there be left over for him to eat? ($7 \div 3 = $ __ R __)

**1477.** What is $26 \div 6$?

**1478.** What is $246 \div 2$?

**1479.** What is $246 \div 3$? ($24 \div 3 =$ __, $6 \div 3 =$ __)

**1480.** What is $963 \div 3$? ($9 \div 3 =$ __, $6 \div 3 =$ __, $3 \div 3 =$ __)

**1481.** What is a related multiplication fact for $24 \div 8 = 3$?

**1482.** What is $180 \div 3$?

**1483.** What is $6000 \div 100$?

**1484.** What is $83 \div 10$? __ Remainder ___

**1485.** Is 21 ÷ 3 greater than, less than, or equal to 8?

**1486.** Is 24 ÷8 greater than, less than, or equal to 2?

**1487.** Is 32 ÷ 4 greater than, less than, or equal to 6?

**1488.** Can you divide bigger numbers on paper using long division?

**1489.** What is the type of math called in which letters and symbols are used to represent an unknown number?

**1490.** What is the value of **a + 5** if **a** = 15?

**1491.** Using the order of operations and doing what is in parenthesis first, how would you simplify the following equation: 8÷(4 ÷ 2) in parenthesis, + 3?

**1492.** How would you solve for **a** if **a** x 5 = 30: **a** = ___?

**1493.** Are you able to read a graph and coordinates?

**1494.** Are you able to read and interpret data on tables, lines, and graphs?

**1495.** What is the missing number in the pattern: 1, 3, 6, 12, ___?

**1496.** What is the missing number in the pattern: 1, 2, ___, 8, 16?

**1497.** What is the next number in the sequence: 1, 3, 6, 10, ___?

**1498.** What is the name of the currency that we use in the United States?

**1499.** Can you name some currencies that are used in other countries?

**1500.** Can you describe the symbol we use for the dollar?

**1501.** Can you describe the symbol we use for cents?

**1502.** Which has a higher value: four quarters or $1.25?

**1503.** Which has the highest value: two twenty dollar bills; a ten, and a five; or a fifty dollar bill?

**1504.** What would $489 be rounded to the nearest ten?

**1505.** What would $489 be rounded to the nearest 100?

**1506.** What would $29.99 be rounded to the nearest ten?

**1507.** When we make purchases, do we have of allow extra for tax in our state?

**1508.** What is the total of 25 cents plus 50 cents plus 10 cents?

**1509.** If Jake raised $22, Megan raised $12, and Cole raised $11 selling raffle tickets, how much money did they raise all together?

**1510.** If you and two friends just bought a pizza for $21.00 and you divided the cost evenly, how much would each of you pay?

**1511.** How much change did Erin receive if she bought a bag of apples for $4.49 and she paid with a ten dollar bill? (Round 49 to __, subtract from 10.)

**1512.** How much would Brianna pay if she bought 4 notebooks that cost 2 dollars each?

**1513.** How much would Eli pay if he bought 2 packs of baseball cards that cost $2.40 each?

**1514.** What is the *unit price* of undershirts if a 3-pack costs $12.00?

**1515.** Which President is on the front of a one-dollar bill: George Washington or Abraham Lincoln?

**1516.** Which President is on the front of a five-dollar bill: George Washington or Abraham Lincoln?

**1517.** Which President is on the front of a ten-dollar bill: Alexander Hamilton or Abraham Lincoln?

**1518.** Which President is on the front of a twenty-dollar bill: Alexander Hamilton or Andrew Jackson?

**1519.** Which President is on the front of a fifty-dollar bill: Ulysses S. Grant or Alexander Hamilton?

**1520.** Which President is on the front of a penny: George Washington or Abraham Lincoln?

**1521.** Which President is on the front of a nickel: Abraham Lincoln or Thomas Jefferson?

**1522.** Which President is on the front of a dime: Franklin D. Roosevelt or Harry Truman?

**1523.** Who is the president on the front of a quarter: George Washington or Abraham Lincoln?

**1524.** What are the units of time, smallest to largest, starting with seconds and going up to one year?

**1525.** How many days are equal to one year?

**1526.** How do we accommodate the extra ¼ day that we have each year?

**1527.** If there are 365 days in one year, how many days are in ½ year?

**1528.** How many hours are there in one day?

**1529.** How many hours are there in ½ a day?

**1530.** How many hours are there in ¼ of a day?

**1531.** How many hours are there in ¾ of a day?

**1532.** How many seconds are there in one minute?

**1533.** How many minutes are there in one hour?

**1534.** How many hours would 90 minutes be equal to?

**1535.** How many minutes in ½ hour?

**1536.** How many minutes in ¼ hour?

**1537.** How many minutes would 5 quarter hours be equal to?

**1538.** How many minutes would there be in 3 hours and 12 minutes? (3 x 60 + 12)

**1539.** How many minutes and seconds would there be in 124 seconds? (124 ÷ 60)

**1540.** How many minutes are there in 2 ¼ hours? (2 x 60 + 15)

**1541.** If you went two camp for 3 weeks, how many days would you be there?

**1542.** What do "Pacific, Mountain, Central, and Eastern refer to with regard to time?

**1543.** What is the name of the time zone that you live in?

**1544.** Are television shows on at different times, depending on the time zone they are broadcast in?

**1545.** If it is now 8:25, what time will it be in one hour?

**1546.** What is another way of saying 9:40?

**1547.** If Callie started her test at 1:45 and finished 40 minutes later, what time did she finish?

**1548.** If the bus trip to Chicago is 8 ½ hours long and it leaves at 10:00 a.m., what time will arrive at its destination?

**1549.** Do you know how to read a transportation schedule in an airport or a train station?

**1550.** What measurement system is used in the United States: the metric system or U.S. customary units?

**1551.** What are the U.S. customary units of measurements smallest to largest, starting with inches?

**1552.** How many inches are in one foot?

**1553.** What fractions of an inch are also indicated on a ruler or measuring instrument?

**1554.** What can we do to approximate the measurement of something?

**1555.** How many feet are in one yard?

**1556.** How many feet are in 1 1/3 yards?

**1557.** How many inches are in one yard?

**1558.** How many inches are in a ½ yard?

**1559.** What customary unit is 5,280 feet long?

**1560.** If 5,280 feet equals one mile, how many feet are there in ½ mile?

**1561.** What customary unit has 1760 yards: a mile or a kilometer?

**1562.** What is the sum of 2 feet 6 inches plus 3 feet 6 inches?

**1563.** What are the U.S. customary units of weight smallest to largest, starting with ounces?

**1564.** How many ounces are there in 1 pound: 16 or 24?

**1565.** How many ounces are there in ½ pound?

**1566.** How many ounces are there in ¾ pound?

**1567.** How many ounces are there in 2 pounds?

**1568.** What customary unit do we often use to estimate weight: pounds or ounces?

**1569.** How many pounds would 48 ounces be equal to?

**1570.** What is the abbreviation of ounce?

**1571.** What is the abbreviation of pound?

**1572.** How many pounds equal one ton: 2000 or 3000?

**1573.** What U.S. customary unit would 6,000 pounds be equal to?

**1574.** What is the abbreviation for ton: t or tn?

**1575.** If a truck weighs 3 ½ tons, how many pounds does it weigh?

**1576.** What are the U.S. customary units for volume, smallest to largest, starting with one cup?

**1577.** What are the U.S. customary units of cooking, smallest to largest, starting with the teaspoon?

**1578.** How many teaspoons are equal to one tablespoon?

**1579.** What is the abbreviation for teaspoon?

**1580.** What is the abbreviation for tablespoon?

**1581.** How many fluid ounces are equal to 1 cup: 4 or 8?

**1582.** What is the abbreviation in a recipe for cup?

**1583.** When we measure volume when we cook, what are the common sizes of cups?

**1584.** How many fluid ounces are equal to one cup: 8 or 16?

**1585.** How many cups are there in one pint: 2 or 4?

**1586.** What is the abbreviation for pint?

**1587.** How many pints are there in one quart: ½ or 2?

**1588.** What is the abbreviation for quart?

**1589.** How many quarts are there in one gallon: 2 or 4?

**1590.** Which is larger: 3 pints or 4 cups?

**1591.** How many tablespoons are equal to 3 tablespoons and 1 teaspoon?

**1592.** What unit of measurement is used in many other countries?

**1593.** What system meaning "ten" is the Metric system based on?

**1594.** What number is associated with **dec**imal, **dec**agon, and **dec**ade?

**1595.** What number is associated with **cen**timeter, **cen**tipede, **cen**tury, and **cen**tennial?

**1596.** What number is associated with **mill**imeter, **mill**ipede, and **mill**ennium?

**1597.** How many millimeters equals one centimeter: 100 or 10?

**1598.** If a caterpillar is 32 millimeters long, how long is it in centimeters?

**1599.** What is the abbreviation for centimeter?

**1600.** What is the abbreviation for millimeter?

**1601.** How many centimeters are equal to one meter: 100 or 1000?

**1602.** What is the abbreviation for meter?

**1603.** Which is longer: a meter or a yard?

**1604.** How many meters are there in one kilometer: 100 or 1000?

**1605.** What is the abbreviation for kilometer?

**1606.** Which is longer: a kilometer or a mile?

**1607.** How many miles is 100 kilometers equal to: 620 or 62?

**1608.** What is the metric unit for measuring liquid capacity: liter or gram?

**1609.** How many centiliters are there in one liter: 10 or 100

**1610.** How many milliliters are there in one liter: 100 or 1000?

**1611.** What is the abbreviation for centiliters?

**1612.** What is the abbreviation for liter?

**1613.** If you and a friend had a one liter bottle of chocolate milk, and you both drank half of it, how many milliliters would you have left: 500 or 1000?

**1614.** What are the metric units of weight smallest to largest: the gram, kilogram, milligram and metric ton?

**1615.** How many grams are equal to one kilogram: 100 or 1000?

**1616.** How many milligrams are there in one centigram: 10 or 100?

**1617.** What is the abbreviation for milligram?

**1618.** What is the abbreviation for centigram?

**1619.** How many milligrams are there in one gram: 100 or 1000?

**1620.** What is the abbreviation for gram?

**1621.** How many centigrams are there in one gram: 100 or 1000?

**1622.** What is the abbreviation for kilogram?

**1623.** Which unit of measurement is used to conduct most science experiments: the U.S. customary system or the metric system?

**1624.** What is the metric unit of measurement for temperature: Celsius or Fahrenheit?

**1625.** What is the U.S. Customary unit of measurement for temperature?

**1626.** If it is 32 degrees Fahrenheit, what is the temperature in degrees Celsius?

**1627.** Is 0 degrees Celsius or 32 degrees Fahrenheit the temperature in which water melts or freezes?

**1628.** What do we call the numbers that are greater than zero but less than one?

**1629.** What is the numerator in the fraction 2/3?

**1630.** What is the denominator in the fraction 4/10?

**1631.** What can 2/4 be reduced to in lowest terms: ½ or ¾?

**1632.** What is the simplest form of the fraction 4/16?

**1633.** Are 1/3 and 3/6 equivalent fractions?

**1634.** What is the equivalent fraction of ¾?

**1635.** What is the equivalent fraction of 1/3?

**1636.** Which fraction is equal to 6/10: ¾ or 3/5?

**1637.** What fraction comes next in the pattern: ½, 2/4, 3/6, ___?

**1638.** Is 9/6 considered a proper or an improper fraction?

**1639.** When the numerator is the same number as the denominator, what number is that fraction equal to?

**1640.** What kind of a fraction is it if the numerator is larger than the denominator: mixed or improper?

**1641.** If you have the fraction 10/5, is that the same as 10 ÷ 5?

**1642.** What is an improper fraction that can be divide evenly with no remainder equal to: a whole number or a mixed fraction?

**1643.** What is 12/3 equal to as a whole number?

**1644.** What whole number is 3/3 equal to?

**1645.** What is 0/8 equal to?

**1646.** What math operation is a bar in a fraction equal to: division or multiplication?

**1647.** Can the fraction 4/10 be reduced?

**1648.** Do you need to divide both the numerator and the denominator by a common factor to reduce a fraction to its lowest terms?

**1649.** What is 4/16 in lowest terms?

**1650.** What is 18/24 in lowest terms?

**1651.** What do we call a number that has both a whole number and a fraction like 1 1/3: mixed or improper?

**1652.** How can the improper fraction 12/5 be written as a mixed number? (12 ÷ 5 = 2 R2)

**1653.** How would you write the mixed number 6 ¼ as an improper fraction: multiply 4 x 6 plus 1 over 4 or, add 6 + 1 over 4?

**1654.** How would you write the mixed number 4 and 2/3 as an improper fraction? (3 x 4 + 2)

**1655.** What number is ½ of 12?

**1656.** What number is 1/3 of 18?

**1657.** What number is ¼ of 16?

**1658.** How do we add fractions with common denominators: by adding or multiplying the numerators?

**1659.** What is the sum of 3/5 + 1/5?

**1660.** What is the sum of 4/9 + 8/9?

**1661.** What is the sum of 2/10 + 3/10 + 5/10?

**1662.** How would you write 12/9 as a mixed number in its lowest terms?

**1663.** What is 5/7 – 3/7?

**1664.** How do you add fractions with unlike denominators: find the least common denominator first, or simply add the original denominators together?

**1665.** What is the sum of ½ and 1/3? (3/6 + 2/6=_)

**1666.** How do you subtract fractions with unlike denominators: find the least common denominator first, or simply subtract the original denominators together?

**1667.** What is ½ - 1/6 reduced to simple terms? (3/6 – 1/6 =_)

**1668.** What is 7/9 – 3/9?

**1669.** If Alegra and Eva picked 2 pounds of strawberries and they ate ½ pound of them, how many pounds of strawberries do they have left?

**1670.** What is the sum of 1 and 1/3 + 1 and 1/3?

**1671.** If Sam is 5 ½ feet tall and Jordan is 3 ½ feet tall, how much taller is Sam than Jordan?

**1672.** If Sofia is 4 ½ feet tall and her sister Isabella is 4 feet tall, how much taller is Sofia than Isabella?

**1673.** If Sofia is ½ foot taller than Isabella, how much taller is she is inches?

**1674.** Is 2/5 + 1/5 greater than, less than, or equal to 4/5?

**1675.** Is 1/3/ + 1/3 greater than, less than, or equal to 2/3?

**1676.** Is ¼ + ¾ greater than, less than, or equal to 1?

**1677.** When following recipes, is it a good idea to use measuring cups and measuring spoons?

**1678.** What is the order smallest to largest of the following measuring cups: ½ 1/3, ¼, and 1?

**1679.** What is the order smallest to largest of the following teaspoons: ¼, 1/8, ½, and 1?

**1680.** If Sarah's class has 12 boys and 12 girls, how much of the class is made up of girls?

**1681.** What fraction would indicate how many of the fish are blue if there are 100 tropical fish in the aquarium, 75 are gold, and 25 are blue: ½, ¼, 2/3, or ¾?

**1682.** What is the product when you multiply the fraction ½ x 3?

**1683.** What is the product when you multiply 2/3 x 1/3?

**1684.** What is the product when you multiply ½ x 2/5?

**1685.** If a candy bar costs one quarter or 25 cents, and there are four quarters in one dollar, what part of a dollar is 25 cents?

**1686.** What fraction of a dollar is fifty cents?

**1687.** What fraction of a dollar is 75 cents?

**1688.** How do we indicate dollars and cents: with decimals or with commas?

**1689.** What is $4.00 + $2.75?

**1690.** What is $4.00 - $2.75?

**1691.** What number is the decimal system based on?

**1692.** What do we call the time span of ten years?

**1693.** How would you write two dollars and fifty cents using a decimal point?

**1694.** How is the fraction 1/10 written as a decimal?

**1695.** How is the fraction 1/100 written as a decimal?

**1696.** How is the fraction 1/1000 written as a decimal?

1697. Is 1.2 greater than, less than, or equal to 1.20?

1698. Are the decimals .9 and .90 equivalent?

1699. Is .9 greater than, less than, or equal to .09?

1700. How would you write the fraction two and four tenths as a decimal?

1701. How would point two five be written as a fraction?

1702. How would point seven five be written as a fraction?

1703. How would point five zero be written as a fraction?

1704. In the number 0.5, which digit is in the ones place?

1705. What would 3.273 be rounded to the nearest tenth if you consider the number to the right of 2?

1706. What would 4.86 be rounded to the nearest tenth if you consider the number to the right of 8?

1707. What would 4.83 be rounded to the nearest tenth if you consider the number to the right of 8?

1708. What would 3.263 be rounded to the nearest hundredth if you consider the number to the right of 2?

1709. What would 3.457 be rounded to the nearest hundredth if you consider the number to the right of 4?

1710. What would 3.248 be rounded to the nearest tenth if you consider the number to the right of 4?

1711. What is 5.612 rounded to the nearest whole number?

1712. Can you read decimals on a number line?

1713. What decimal would come next in the sequence: 1.5, 1.6, 1.7, __?

1714. What do you have to line up when you are adding decimals together: whole numbers or decimal points?

1715. What number do you need to add to 1.2 to make it line up evenly with 1.35 before you add them together?

1716. Can you *estimate* the sum of the following by rounding each number to the nearest whole number, and then adding them together: 4.8 + 2.1 = ___?

1717. What is the sum of 1.5 + 1.4?

1718. What is the sum of 2.5 + 2.5?

1719. If Andrew watched his turtle move 0.2 centimeters, then move 0.4 centimeters more, and then 0.3 centimeters more, how much distance did his turtle travel in all?

1720. Is 5/4 greater than, less than, or equal to 1.25?

1721. What is the study of points, lines, segments, and shapes called?

1722. Which can go on infinitely: a line or a line segment?

**1723.** What symbols are line segments often labeled with: letters or numbers?

**1724.** What do we draw at either end of a line to show that it can go on forever in either direction?

**1725.** What is the name of a line that has one end point and an arrow pointing in one direction: a segment or a ray?

**1726.** What point to we start with when we are labeling a ray: the end point or the point closer to the arrow?

**1727.** What is formed when two rays have the same end point: an angle or a line segment?

**1728.** What is another name for the end point: the axis or the vertex?

**1729.** How many sides does a triangle have?

**1730.** What is the name of an angle that forms a square corner?

**1731.** How many degrees does a right angle measure: 45 or 90?

**1732.** What is the name of an angle that is *less* than a right angle: acute or obtuse?

**1733.** What is the name of an angle that is *greater* than a right angle: acute or obtuse?

**1734.** Can we help ourselves remember the difference between *a*cute and *o*btuse if we think that "**a**" is a lower (or lesser) letter than "**o**" which is 'higher' in the alphabet?

**1735.** What is the name of a triangle that has *two* sides that are equal: isosceles or equilateral?

**1736.** If you have a triangle with each angle measuring 60 degrees, what kind of triangle is it: isosceles or equilateral?

**1737.** What is the name of a triangle that has 3 sides with different lengths: isosceles or scalene?

**1738.** If a triangle has one angle that measures 90 degrees, what kind of triangle is it: equilateral or right?

**1739.** What is the name of the tool you can use similar to a ruler for measuring angles: a protractor or a compass?

**1740.** If an angle measures 80 degrees and part of the angle measures 30 degrees, what is the measurement of the *adjacent* angle? (80-30= ___)

**1741.** How many degrees is ½ turn of an angle: 90 or 180?

**1742.** How many degrees is ¼ turn of an angle: 45 or 90?

**1743.** How many degrees is ¾ turn of an angle: 180 or 270?

**1744.** How many degrees is 1 full turn of an angle: 270 or 360?

**1745.** What do we call two lines when they cross each other: intersecting or parallel?

**1746.** What do we call two lines that intersect each other and form right angles: perpendicular or parallel?

1747. What do we call lines that always stay the same distance apart and never intersect: perpendicular or parallel?

1748. What are lines called that run east and west like the "horizon?"

1749. What are lines called that run up and down or north and south?

1750. What are lines called that run northeast to southwest or join two opposite vertices of a quadrilateral?

1751. What is the general term of a closed plane shape with three or more line segments and angles: a polygon or a hexagon?

1752. What is the name of a polygon that is three-sided?

1753. What is the name of a polygon that has four sides: a quadrilateral or a diagonal?

1754. What two quadrilateral shapes have *two* pairs of parallel lines?

1755. What is the name of a quadrilateral with sides that run parallel: a parallelogram or a matrix?

1756. What is a quadrilateral called that has *one* pair of parallel lines: a trapezoid or a rhombus?

1757. What is a rectangle called that has four sides that are all the same exact length?

1758. What is a diamond an example of: a rhombus or a trapezoid?

1759. What is the name of any polygon with four sides: a square or a quadrilateral?

1760. What is the name of a polygon with five sides: a pentagon or a hexagon?

1761. What is the name of a polygon with six sides: a pentagon or a hexagon?

1762. What is the name of the polygon with seven sides: a hexagon or a heptagon?

1763. What is the name of a polygon with eight sides: a hexagon or an octagon?

1764. What is the name of a polygon with nine sides: a decagon or a nonagon?

1765. What is the name of a polygon with ten sides: a decagon or a pentagon?

1766. What animal are you familiar with that has 8 "arms?"

1767. Which polygon is the shape of a red stop sign?

1768. What is the name of a polygon that has 4 straight lines of equal lengths but the lines do not form right angles: a rhombus or a trapezoid?

1769. What are shapes called that have the same shape and the same size: congruent or similar?

1770. What are shapes called that have the same shape but are *not* the same size: congruent or similar?

1771. What is a shape called that has matching points on both sides of a line dividing it, and if you folded it in half, it would match up exactly: symmetrical or asymmetrical?

1772. What part of a shape would a line of symmetry run through?

1773. If you multiply the length times the width of a square or a rectangle, what would you be measuring: area or perimeter?

1774. If a rectangle measures 8 centimeters long and 4 centimeters wide, what is its area?

1775. If a square measures 3 feet by 3 feet, what is its area?

1776. Do we measure area in square units?

1777. If there are 12 inches in one foot, how many inches are there in 1 square foot? (12x12=__)

1778. What are some examples of U.S. customary units of area besides square inch?

1779. What are some examples of metric units of area besides square millimeter?

1780. Are polygons 2 or 3 dimensional?

1781. Can 2-dimensional shapes be drawn on a plane?

1782. What is the name of the **3**-dimensional shape that often has a triangular or rectangular base, and can break light into the colors of the spectrum?

1783. What is the name of the **3**-dimensional shape that has two flat circular ends and is shaped like a tube?

1784. What is the name of the **3**-dimensional shape that often has a polygon base and sides that are triangular that meet to form a point at the top, and is also the name for the buildings that the ancient Egyptians and Maya built?

1785. What is the name of the **3**-dimensional shape that has no flat surfaces and all points of the shape are the same distance from the center of the shape, similar to a globe?

1786. What is the name of the **3**-dimensional shape that has 6 square faces, similar to dice?

1787. What is the name of the **3**-dimensional shape that has a base that is round and a point at the top, similar to what you crunch on under your scoop of ice cream?

1788. What part of a 3-dimensional shape includes the top, bottom, left, right, front, and back: the perimeter or the surface area?

1789. Can you count the sides, edges, vertices, and faces on geometric figures?

1790. When we measure the amount of space or cubic units that a 3 dimensional figure takes up, what are we measuring: the surface area or the volume?

1791. If a rectangular prism has 6 cubes on one layer and there are 2 layers, how many cubic centimeters are in the prism?

1792. Is a circle a polygon?

1793. What is the name of the tool you can use to draw a circle: a compass or a protractor?

**1794.** What is it called when you draw a straight line from the center of a circle to any point on the outer edge of the circle: diameter or radius?

**1795.** What is it called when you draw a straight line from one point on the circle, through the center of the circle to the opposite end point: diameter or radius?

**1796.** What is it called when you draw a straight line that join two points on a curve of a circle: chord or arc?

**1797.** Which is longer: the radius or the diameter?

**1798.** What can you adjust on a compass to determine the size of the circle: the radius or the diameter?

**1799.** If the radius of a circle is 8 centimeters, what is its diameter: 16 or 64?

**1800.** What is the distance around a circle called: its radius or its circumference?

**1801.** Can you make a prediction about something?

**1802.** If a spinner has 4 blue sections, 3 red sections, and 2 yellow sections, which color would you predict that the arrow is most likely to land when you spin it?

**1803.** If you flipped a quarter 8 times, how many times would you predict that the quarter will land on "heads?"

**1804.** When we want to find the average of different numbers, what do we need to do after we add them together?

**1805.** What is the average of the numbers 2, 4, and 6?

**1806.** If you scored a 10 on your spelling test, your friend Emily scored a 7, and your friend Avery also scored a 7, what is the average score? ($10+7+7 \div 3 = \_$)

**1807.** If you have a set of numbers from smallest to largest, what is the number located in the middle called: the mean, the mode, the median, or the range?

**1808.** What is the mean or average value of the following numbers: 2, 3, 5, and 6? ($2+3+5+6 \div 4 = \_$)

**1809.** If you have a set of numbers, what is the number called that is listed most frequently: the mean, the mode, the median, or the range?

**1810.** What is the mode in the following set of numbers: 1, 3, 3, 4, 5, 3, 6, 3?

**1811.** If you have a set of numbers and you want to find the average of those numbers, what would you be finding: the mean, the mode, the median, or the range?

**1812.** What is the mean in the following set of numbers: 1, 3, 4, 4? ($1+3+4+4 \div 4 = \_$)

**1813.** What are you finding if you have a set of numbers written in random order, and you subtract the smallest value that is listed from the largest value listed: the mean, the mode, the median, or the range?

**1814.** What is the range of the following set of numbers: 0, 1, 5, 4, and 3?

## Math – 5th Grade

**1815.** What big number comes after a million that has 9 zeros in it?

**1816.** What symbol do we use to indicate the place value of thousands, millions, and billions?

**1817.** How many place values do you count back from the end of the number before inserting a comma?

**1818.** How many zeros are there in one hundred thousand: 100,000?

**1819.** How many zeros are there in one million: 1,000,000?

**1820.** How many zeros are there in ten million: 10,000,000?

**1821.** How many zeros are there in one hundred million: 100,000,000?

**1822.** How many zeros are there in one billion: 1,000,000,000?

**1823.** How would you write the number six hundred and twelve billion?

**1824.** How would you write the number five thousand four hundred eighty using digits?

**1825.** What is the sum of: 50,000 + 3,000 + 900 + 20 + 7?

**1826.** What is the number 8,145 in expanded form: 8000 + _?

**1827.** What is the place value of 9 in the number 9,876,543,210: 9 billion or 9 million?

**1828.** What is the place value of 8 in the number 9,876,543,210: 800 million or 80 million?

**1829.** What is the place value of 7 in the number 9,876,543,210: 70 thousand or 70 million?

**1830.** What is the place value of 6 in the number 9,876,543,210: 6 million or 600 thousand?

**1831.** What is the place value of 5 in the number 9,876,543,210: 500 thousand or 50 thousand?

**1832.** What is the place value of 4 in the number 9,876,543,210: 400 thousand or 40 thousand?

**1833.** What is the place value of 3 in the number 9,876,543,210: 3 thousand or 30 thousand?

**1834.** What is the place value of 2 in the number 9,876,543,210: 2 hundred or 2 thousand?

**1835.** What is the place value of 1 in the number 9,876,543,210: tens or ones?

**1836.** What is the place value of 0 in the number 9,876,543,210: tens or ones?

**1837.** When do we use Roman numerals?

**1838.** What does the letter "V" represent as a Roman numeral: 5 or 10?

**1839.** What does the letter "X" represent as a Roman numeral: 10 or 50?

**1840.** What does the letter "L" represent as a Roman numeral: 50 or 500?

**1841.** What does the letter "C" represent as a Roman numeral: 100 or 1000?

**1842.** What does the letter "D" represent as a Roman numeral: 500 or 50?

**1843.** What does the letter "M" represent as a Roman numeral: 100 or 1000?

**1844.** What number would Roman numeral CLXXVI be equal to in Arabic numbers: 100 + 50 + 20 +6?

**1845.** What number would Roman numeral LXXVI be equal to in Arabic numbers: L = 50 +20 +6?

**1846.** What number would Roman numeral MDCLXXXVI be: 1000 + 500 + 100 + 50 + 30 + 5 + 1?

**1847.** If M = 1000, how would you write three thousand five using Roman numerals?

**1848.** What digit do you look at to round a number to a certain place: the digit to the right or to the left of that place value?

**1849.** Are Roman numerals often used when writing an outline?

**1850.** What does the number have to be, or be higher than in order to round up that number?

**1851.** What would the number 9,821,000 be, rounded to the nearest million?

**1852.** What would the number 9,432,000 be, rounded to the nearest million?

**1853.** What would the number 3,946,000 be, rounded to the nearest hundred thousand?

**1854.** What would the number 3,421,000 be, rounded to the nearest hundred thousand?

**1855.** What would the number 3,946,000 be, rounded to the nearest ten thousand?

**1856.** What would the number 3,421,000 be, rounded to the nearest ten thousand?

**1857.** What would the number 2,689 be, rounded to the nearest thousand?

**1858.** What would the number 2,489 be, rounded to the nearest thousand?

**1859.** What would the number 59,853 be, rounded to the nearest thousand?

**1860.** What would the number 45,325 be, rounded to the nearest thousand?

**1861.** What would the number 45,526 be, rounded to the nearest thousand?

**1862.** What would the number 45,526 be, rounded to the nearest hundred?

**1863.** What would the number 45,587 be, rounded to the nearest hundred?

**1864.** What would the number 5,526 be, rounded to the nearest ten?

**1865.** What would the number 5,587 be, rounded to the nearest ten?

**1866.** What would the number 421 be, rounded to the nearest one?

**1867.** What would the number 425 be, rounded to the nearest one?

**1868.** Is the sum of 20 + 21 even or odd?

**1869.** Is the difference of 20 – 12 even or odd?

**1870.** Is the product of 8 x 9 even or odd?

**1871.** Is the quotient of 28 ÷4 even or odd?

**1872.** What is another term for *whole* numbers: fractions or integers?

**1873.** Is the number zero considered an integer?

**1874.** Is a *positive* number always greater than or less than a negative number?

**1875.** Are integers often written on a number line with *zero* in the middle?

**1876.** Are numbers that are the same distance from zero on a number line in opposite directions called distant numbers or opposite numbers?

**1877.** Do integers lose value or gain value as you move farther to the right on the number line?

**1878.** Do integers lose value or gain value as you move farther to the left on a number line?

**1879.** If the temperature is 5 degrees above zero, is that a positive number or a negative number?

**1880.** If the temperature is 5 degrees below zero, is that a positive number or a negative number?

**1881.** Are the numbers to the right of 0 on a number line positive or negative?

**1882.** Are the numbers to the left of 0 on a number line positive or negative?

**1883.** What do we write before a number to show that it is negative?

**1884.** Is it always necessary to write a *plus* sign before a positive number?

**1885.** Are the numbers +2 and –2 considered likes or opposites?

**1886.** What is the opposite of –5?

**1887.** What is the opposite of +7?

**1888.** What is the opposite of -20?

**1889.** Which integer represents winning $10 in a raffle: +10 or –10?

**1890.** Which integer represents earning $25 for working in the yard: +25 or –25?

**1891.** Which integer represents spending $5 for a turkey sandwich: +5 or –5?

**1892.** Which integer represents a gain of 10 yards in a football game: +10 or –10?

**1893.** Which integer represents a loss of 15 yards in a football game: +15 or –15?

**1894.** How would you indicate that a sunken pirate ship from long ago was located 200 meters below sea level?

**1895.** Which integer represents losing 4 pounds: +4 or –4 (negative 4)?

**1896.** Is the integer –1 greater than, less than, or equal to +1?

**1897.** Is the integer –1 greater than, less than, or equal to 0?

**1898.** Is the integer –1 greater than, less than, or equal to –3?

**1899.** Is the integer 1 greater than, less than, or equal to –1?

**1900.** Is the integer –8 greater than, less than, or equal to –4?

**1901.** Is the integer –4 greater than, less than, or equal to –8?

**1902.** Can we add and subtract integers?

**1903.** Is the sum of two positive integers positive or negative?

**1904.** If you are adding positive integers, in what direction do you move on a number line: to the right or to the left?

**1905.** Is the sum of two negative integers positive or negative?

**1906.** If you are adding negative integers do you keep moving to the right or to the left on the number line?

**1907.** What is the sum of 2 + 4?

**1908.** Can the sum of positive 2 plus positive 4 be written 2 + 4?

**1909.** What is the sum of -3 + (-2), if you start at –3 on the number line and then move 2 more units to the left?

**1910.** What is the sum of -10 + 6, if you start at –10 on a number line and then move 6 units to the right?

**1911.** What is the sum of -60 + 20?

**1912.** What is the sum of –20 + 25?

**1913.** Is the sum of opposites the same?

**1914.** What is the opposite of -10 + 6?

**1915.** What would be the sum of the opposite of 10 + (-4)?

**1916.** What is the sum of -5 +5?

**1917.** What is the sum of -27 + 27?

**1918.** Is the sum of an integer and its exact opposite zero?

**1919.** Can you also subtract integers?

**1920.** Is subtracting an integer the same as adding or subtracting its opposite?

**1921.** Is 5 –7 the same as 5 + (-7)?

**1922.** What is -2 – (-4), (Negative two minus negative four), if we add its opposite (-2 + 4)?

**1923.** What is -7 – (-4), (Negative seven minus negative four), if we add its opposite (-7 + 4)?

**1924.** What is 9 – 3, if we add its opposite (9 + -3)?

**1925.** Do you remember your times tables? (2 x 2, 2 x 3…)

**1926.** When you *square* a number, what do you multiply a number by: 2 or itself?

**1927.** What is the square of 2?

**1928.** Is 2 squared equal to 4 because 2 x 2 = 4?

**1929.** What is the square of 3?

**1930.** Can we say that 3 squared equals 9?

**1931.** What is the square root of 4?

**1932.** What is the square root of 9?

**1933.** What is the square root of 16?

**1934.** What is the square root of 25?

**1935.** What is the square root of 36?

**1936.** What is the square root of 49?

**1937.** What is 6 squared?

**1938.** What is 7 squared?

**1939.** What is the square root of 64?

**1940.** What is 9 squared?

**1941.** What is 10 squared?

**1942.** What is the square root of 144?

**1943.** When we write 4 squared, or 4 to the second power, are we using integers or exponents?

**1944.** What is the definition of an exponent: a small number raised up that represents how many times a number is multiplied, or the base number that is written in normal size?

**1945.** How would you factor the number 2 to the third power?

**1946.** Is the number 5 to the third power regarded as 5 cubed or 5 squared?

**1947.** How would 5 x 5 x 5 x 5 be written as an exponent?

**1948.** What is 9 to the first power equal to?

**1949.** What is 10 to the third power (10 cubed) equal to: (10 x 10 x 10)?

**1950.** If you take 10 to the fifth power, can you write its equivalent simply by writing a one with 5 zeros?

**1951.** How many zeros would 10 to the sixth power have?

**1952.** What number would 10 to the sixth power be: One million or ten million?

**1953.** What would one billion be written as an exponent: 10 to the 8th power, or 10 to the 9th power?

**1954.** What is a number called that cannot be divided evenly by any number except the number itself, or by the number one: a prime number or a multiple number?

**1955.** Are the numbers zero and one considered prime numbers or composite numbers?

**1956.** What is the name of a number divisible by 2: a prime number or a composite number?

**1957.** Is 2 a prime number or a composite number?

**1958.** What are numbers called that are not prime numbers: integers or composite numbers?

**1959.** What is the number 17: prime or composite?

**1960.** What are the numbers called that you can multiply together to arrive at a larger number: multiples or factors?

**1961.** What are all the factors of the number 16?

**1962.** What is prime factor of the number 16: 2 or 4?

**1963.** What is the prime factorization of the number 9?

**1964.** What is the prime factorization of the number 9 written as an exponent?

**1965.** What is the prime factorization of the number 15?

**1966.** What are all the factors of 20 that can by multiplied together to get 20?

**1967.** What is the greatest common factor, the largest factor in common between the numbers of 6 and 9?

**1968.** What is the greatest common factor of 6 and 8?

**1969.** What is the greatest common factor of 27 and 36?

**1970.** If multiples of 2 include 2, 4, 6, and 8, and multiples of 3 include 3, 6, 9, and 12, what is the least common multiple (LCM) of the numbers 2 and 3: 6 or 12?

**1971.** What is the least common multiple (LCM) of 4 and 8: 16 or 24?

**1972.** Do you remember your addition facts?

**1973.** What is the sum of 9,000 + 12,000?

**1974.** Which property of addition is demonstrated in 2 + 3 =5 and 3 +2 = 5: the commutative or the associative?

**1975.** Which property of addition is demonstrated in (4+ 2) in parenthesis + 3 =9, and 4 + (2 + 3) in parenthesis = 5: the distributive or the associative?

**1976.** Is 54 greater than, less than, or equal to 32 +24?

**1977.** Is 21 greater than, less than, or equal to 13 + 8?

**1978.** Is 81 greater than, less than, or equal to 32 + 47?

**1979.** How would you estimate the sum of 231 +179 to the nearest hundred?

**1980.** Can you add and compare decimals?

**1981.** Which is greater: 3.1 or 3.3?

**1982.** What is greater: .05 or .50?

**1983.** Is 65.450 the same as 65.45?

**1984.** Is .36 greater or less than .036?

**1985.** Can you read .36 as both point three six and 36 hundredths?

**1986.** Is the number 15.53 the same as 15.530?

**1987.** Is 12.425 greater than or less than 12.420?

**1988.** When adding larger decimals, what number can you add to line all the numbers up without changing the value of the number?

**1989.** What is the sum of .2 and .6?

**1990.** How much total snowfall was there if it snowed 1.5 inches in the morning, and another 2.5 inches in the afternoon?

**1991.** What is the name for the branch of mathematics in which relationships and operations are expressed through symbols that represent quantities, usually letters of the alphabet?

**1992.** When we solve an equation, what common symbol is used to stand for a number?

**1993.** What is the letter called in the equation 2 + b = 7: the integer or the variable?

**1994.** How can you solve for the variable y: (.8 – y = .5)?

**1995.** Is .7 + .8 greater than, lesser than, or equal to .15?

**1996.** What is the sum of the following if you round to the nearest whole number and then add: 10.5 + 4.3?

**1997.** What is the opposite operation of addition?

**1998.** What kinds of operations are addition and subtraction: inverse or associative?

**1999.** What is the related *subtraction* fact for 7 + 5 = 12?

**2000.** What is the related *addition* fact for 22 – 8 = 14?

**2001.** Do you remember your subtraction facts?

**2002.** What is the difference of 48 – 9?

**2003.** What is the difference of: 8,000 – 7,100?

**2004.** What is the difference of: 179,000 –78,000?

**2005.** What is difference of $4.75 - $2.25?

**2006.** What is the difference of $50.00 - $24.00?

**2007.** Is 65 – 15 greater than, less than, or equal to 75 - 25?

**2008.** What is the difference of the following if you round to the nearest whole number and then subtract: 56-31?

**2009.** If Elizabeth earned $986 dollars and she spend $235 of it, what is the estimated difference? (986 rounds to __, 235 rounds to __, subtracted equals __)

**2010.** Do you remember your multiplication tables?

**2011.** What is the product of 8 x 9?

**2012.** When multiplying two large numbers, would you add or subtract the zeros?

**2013.** What is the product of 10 x 1000: (One plus four zeros)?

**2014.** What is the product of 7,000 x 6?

**2015.** What is the product of 700 x 500: (35 plus four zeros)?

**2016.** Can you multiply two and three digit numbers on paper?

**2017.** Which property of multiplication is demonstrated in the equations 2 x 3 =6 and 3 x 2 = 6: commutative or associative?

**2018.** Which property of multiplication is demonstrated in (4x 2) in parenthesis x 3 =24 and 4 x (2 x 3) in parenthesis = 24: commutative or associative?

**2019.** Which property of multiplication is demonstrated in 2 x (3 + 4) in parenthesis, is equal to (2 x 3) in parenthesis, + (2 x 4) in parenthesis: associative or distributive?

**2020.** Which property of multiplication is demonstrated in 2 x (4 + 5) in parenthesis, is equal to 2 x 4 + 2 x 5: associative or distributive?

**2021.** Which property of multiplication is demonstrated in the equation 45 x 0 = 0: identity or zero?

**2022.** Which property of multiplication is demonstrated in the equation 7643 x 1 = 7643: identity or zero?

**2023.** What is the product of 3 x 10 x 4?

**2024.** How would you estimate the product of 59 x 33: (60x30)?

**2025.** Is 75 greater than, less than, or equal to 3 x 23?

**2026.** Is 75 greater than, less than, or equal to 3 x 25?

**2027.** What is the product of .7 x .3?

**2028.** When you multiply a decimal by 10, how many places to the right do you place the decimal point: 1 or 2?

**2029.** What is the product of 10 x 8.0

**2030.** What is the product of 10 x 2.325?

**2031.** When you multiply a decimal by 100, how many places to the right do you place the decimal point: 1 or 2?

**2032.** What is the product of 100 x 2.325?

**2033.** If you buy 8 bags of chips that cost .70 cents each, how much would you pay total?

**2034.** How would you estimate the product of 873 x 11: (900 x 10)?

**2035.** How would you estimate the product of 4287 x 489: (4000 x 500)?

**2036.** Is 6.2 greater than, less than, or equal to 2 x 3.1?

**2037.** What is the inverse operation of multiplication?

**2038.** What is the term for the number you are dividing out: the dividend or the divisor?

**2039.** What is the term for the number you are dividing by: the dividend or the divisor?

**2040.** What is the term for the number that represents the answer to a division problem: the product or the quotient?

**2041.** What is the quotient of 66 ÷ 3 = __?

**2042.** What is 144 ÷ 12?

**2043.** What is 77 ÷ 7?

**2044.** What is 1200 ÷ 3?

**2045.** What is the term for the number that is left over after a number is divided out evenly?

**2046.** Can you divide by two and three digits with remainders?

**2047.** When dividing large numbers, can you check your work by multiplying the quotient and the divisor and then adding the remainder?

**2048.** Is 45,000 greater than, less than, or equal to 92,222 ÷2 if you estimate: (90,000 ÷ 2)?

**2049.** What is the quotient of 18.284 ÷ 6 using estimation: (18÷6)?

**2050.** What is the quotient if you estimate 10.39 to the nearest ten divided by one?

**2051.** When you divide a number by 10, how many places do you move the decimal point to the left?

**2052.** What is 483.4 ÷10?

**2053.** When you divide a number by 100, how many places do you move the decimal point to the left?

**2054.** What is 483.4 ÷100?

**2055.** What are the two terms that make up a fraction?

**2056.** Is the denominator the top or bottom part of a fraction?

**2057.** What number of a fraction is the numerator: the top or the bottom?

**2058.** What is the equivalent of ¼: 2/8 or 2/4?

**2059.** How would you reduce 4/8 to its lowest terms?

**2060.** If you divide both the numerator and the denominator by its greatest common factor, what is 12/18 in its lowest terms?

**2061.** What is the greatest common factor or GCM of 12/18: 3 or 6?

**2062.** What do we need to do to find the least common denominator of two fractions: find the least common multiple or LCM of each denominator, or multiply both the numerators and the denominators?

**2063.** What is the least common multiple of 1/3 and 1/6: 3 or 6?

**2064.** What is the least common denominator or LCD of 1/3 and 1/6?

**2065.** What is the least common denominator or LCD of ½ and 1/8?

**2066.** How would you reduce the fraction 8/10 to lowest terms?

**2067.** What would 2 ½ be as an improper fraction: (2x2+1 =__/2)?

**2068.** Does a mixed number include both an integer and a fraction, or just a fraction?

**2069.** What is the *mixed* number of 4/3: 1 and 1/3, or 2 and 1/3?

**2070.** Is 1/3 greater than or less than 2/3?

**2071.** What do we need to find first when comparing fractions that have different denominators: a common denominator or a common numerator?

2072. When comparing the fractions 2/3 and 4/5, do we first need to find the lowest common denominators of 3 and 5?

2073. What is the lowest common multiple or LCM of 1/3 and 1/5: the number 15 or the number 20?

2074. What does the fraction 2/3 convert to if we multiply both the numerator and the denominator by 5: (2x5 and 3x5=__)?

2075. What is the fraction 10/15 in lowest terms?

2076. What does the fraction 4/5 convert to if we multiply both the numerator and the denominator by 3: (4x3 and5x3=__)?

2077. What is the fraction 12/15 in lowest terms?

2078. If 2/3 becomes 10/15, and 4/5 becomes 12/15, which is greater: 2/3 or 4/5?

2079. What is the order of the following fractions least to greatest: ¼, 1/3, 1, ½, and 3/4"?

2080. What is the next fraction in the sequence: 1/3, 1/6, and 1/12?

2081. What is the next fraction in the sequence: 6/7, 5/7, and 4/7?

2082. What is 1 ¾ rounded to the nearest whole number?

2083. What is 90 and 1/6 rounded to the nearest whole number?

2084. How do you get the reciprocal of a fraction: multiply it by 2, or turn it upside down?

2085. What is the reciprocal of 2/5?

2086. What is the reciprocal of 4/3?

2087. What is the sum of 1/3 + 1/3?

2088. What is the sum of 1/3 + 1/3 + 1/3?

2089. What is the sum of 2/9 + 1/9 + 4/9?

2090. If you add 3/7 + 7/7, is it best to write the sum as 10/7, or as the mixed number 1 and 3/7?

2091. What is the sum of 2/3 + 2/3?

2092. How is 4/3 written as a mixed number: 1 and 1/3, or 1 and ¼?

2093. What is the sum of 1 ½ + 1 ½?

2094. What is the sum of 4 and 1/3 + 2 and 1/3?

2095. What is the sum of 2 ¼ + 2 ¼ in lowest terms: 4 and ¼, or 4 and ½?

2096. What is the sum of 10 and 1/6 + 5 and 2/6 in lowest terms? (10 + 5 and 1/6 + 2/6)?

2097. Can you subtract fractions with common denominators?

**2098.** What is the difference of 3/5 – 1/5?

**2099.** What is the difference of 6/8 – 3/8?

**2100.** What is the difference of 2 and 4/5 – 1 and 2/5? (2-1, 4/5 - 2/5)?

**2101.** Can you add and subtract fractions with unlike denominators?

**2102.** If Ben ate 2/8 of the pizza, and Drew ate 3/8 of the pizza, how many pieces were left?

**2103.** What is the missing numerator in the equation 1/8+ __/8 = ½: (1/2 = 4/8 so 1 plus what would equal 4?

**2104.** Is 8/9 greater than, less than, or equal to 4/9 + 3/9?

**2105.** Is 7/8 greater than, less than, or equal to 12/8 – 5/8?

**2106.** Is 3/5 greater than, less than, or equal to 2/5 + 2/5?

**2107.** Can you estimate the difference of the following by rounding to the nearest whole number and then subtracting: 4 and 4/5 - 2 and 1/5? (4 4/5 rounds to __, 2 and 1/5 rounds to __, 5-2=_)

**2108.** Can you estimate the sum of the following by rounding to the nearest whole number and then adding: 3 and 5/8 + 2 and 1/8 = _? (3 and 5/8 rounds to _; 2 and 1/8 rounds to _; 4 + 2 = _)

**2109.** When we multiply fractions by a whole number, do we multiply the denominator by the whole number and then divide by the numerator?

**2110.** Is the equation 1/3 x 6 the same as 1/3 *of* 6?

**2111.** What operation does 1/3 x 6 =2 which is equal to 6 x 1/3 represent: the commutative or the associative operation?

**2112.** What is the product of ¾ x 4? (3 x 4 =_divided by 4 = _)

**2113.** When we multiply fractions do we multiply the numerators and then the denominators?

**2114.** How would you finish the rhyme for multiplying fractions: "Multiplying fractions, no big problem, top times top over bottom times bottom. And don't forget to simplify, before it's time to say _?"

**2115.** What is the product of 1/3 x 1/5?

**2116.** What is the product of 2/3 x 2/5?

**2117.** What is the product of ½ x ½ x ½?

**2118.** What is the product of 2/5 x 2/3?

**2119.** Can you estimate the product by first rounding to the nearest whole number and then multiplying the following equation: 4 and 2/3 x 6 = _? (5x6)

**2120.** What is the product of 1 ¼ x 8? (5/4 x 8 = 40/4 = 10)

**2121.** What is the product of 3 ½ x 4? (3 ½ becomes 7/2; 7/2 x 4 = 28/2, 28 ÷2=_)

**2122.** When we multiply by the reciprocal of a fraction, is that the same as dividing the fraction?

**2123.** What is the improper reciprocal 10/5 the same as: $10 \div$ __?

**2124.** What is the quotient of $\frac{1}{2} \div 2$? ( $\frac{1}{2}$ **x** 2/1=2/2=_)

**2125.** What is the quotient of $1/2 \div 1/6$? ( $\frac{1}{2}$ **x** 6/1 = 6/2 =_)

**2126.** What is the quotient of $1/2 \div 1/3$? ( $\frac{1}{2}$ **x** 3/1 = 3/2 = 1 and__/__)

**2127.** What is the quotient of $1/3 \div 1/3$? (1/3 x 3/1 = 3/3 =_)

**2128.** When comparing the size of two numbers, are you finding the ratio or the percent?

**2129.** How would you read the ratio written as one colon three?

**2130.** If you have 2 stuffed dogs and 5 stuffed elephants, what is the ratio of dogs to elephants?

**2131.** What fraction is equal to the ratio 1 to 4: $\frac{1}{4}$ or $\frac{1}{2}$?

**2132.** How is the ratio 1 to 4 written as a percentage: 25% or 75%?

**2133.** How is the ratio 2 to 1 written as a percentage: 25% or 50%?

**2134.** How is the ratio 3 to 1 written as a percentage: 75% or 30%?

**2135.** Should you write ratios in lowest terms?

**2136.** What is the ratio 6 to 3 in lowest terms?

**2137.** Is the ratio 1 to 2 the same as 2 to 4 or 2 to 1?

**2138.** Is $\frac{1}{2}$ or 1 to 2 the same proportion as 2 /4 or 2 to 4?

**2139.** What is the math term for the comparison of two measurements in which one of the two things has a value of one: a ratio or a unit rate?

**2140.** What is the unit rate of pigs per farm if there are 18 pigs at 3 farms?

**2141.** What is the unit rate of gumballs if 4 gumballs costs one dollar?

**2142.** What does a scale drawing use to represent the size of something: a ratio or a fraction?

**2143.** Would you likely find scale drawings maps and floor plans?

**2144.** If one inch is equal to 5 miles on a city map scale, and the distance from Apple Valley to Pinehurst is 4 inches long, how many miles apart are the two cities?

**2145.** What would be the water to concentrate ratio if you are making lemonade and need to mix 6 cans of water with 1 can of frozen concentrate?

**2146.** What would be the concentrate to water ratio if you are making lemonade and need to mix 6 cans of water with 1 can of frozen concentrate?

**2147.** What would the ratio be if the scale on the blueprints of a house is: 1 inch = 10 feet?

**2148.** What is the ratio called between 2 different quantities: the speed or the rate?

**2149.** Is speed a common form of rate?

**2150.** What is a common speed per hour on the highway?

**2151.** How do you measure the rate of speed using U.S. customary units: in miles or in kilometers?

**2152.** How do you measure the rate of speed using the Metric system?

**2153.** What are you measuring when you multiply the rate by the time: speed or distance?

**2154.** If you travelled by car 180 miles in 3 hours, at what speed did you travel per hour?

**2155.** Is percent considered a ratio?

**2156.** What number does a percent compare a number to: 10 or 100?

**2157.** If "percent" means per 100, what things besides coins ("cents") are related to the number 100 and begin with "cent?"

**2158.** What is 30% equal to: 30 out of 100, or 3 out of 10?

**2159.** How would 30% be written as a fraction?

**2160.** What percent is equal to ¼?

**2161.** What percent is equal to ½?

**2162.** What percent is equal to ¾?

**2163.** What percent is equal to the whole number 1?

**2164.** What fraction is 50% equal to?

**2165.** What fraction is 75% equal to?

**2166.** What fraction is 25% equal to?

**2167.** What fraction is 100% equal to?

**2168.** How would you write 75% as a decimal?

**2169.** How would you write 25% as a decimal?

**2170.** How would you write 50% as a decimal?

**2171.** If ¼ of the pizza had black olives, what percentage of the pizza was covered with olives?

**2172.** If the family ate 6 out of the 8 slices of pie for dessert, what percentage of the pie is left?

**2173.** What is the percentage of the following: 0.6 = 0.60 = 60/100 = _?

2174. How do you find the percent of a number: multiply or divide?

2175. If there are 200 students in the school, and 20% of them are in fifth grade, how many total students are in fifth grade? (.20 x 200=_)

2176. What is 40% of 60? ( .40 x 60= _)

2177. If a jacket you like in the store has a price tag of $40, and there is a sale offering 20% off, how much will the jacket cost you after the discount? (40 x .20 = _, $40 - $8 = __)

2178. What is the mathematical term used to describe how likely it is that some particular thing will happen: probability or possibility?

2179. Is there a fifty-fifty chance that if you flip a coin it will land on "heads?"

2180. What is the probability of any one number turning up when throwing a single die: 1 in 5 or 1 in 6?

2181. What is the common phrase of probability when it is extremely remote that something will happen, like winning the lottery? (One in a __!)

2182. If you have a bag of candy with 3 red mints and 1 white mint, what is the probability that you will pick out the white mint?

2183. What is the probability that you will pick a red mint?

2184. How can one in four be written as a fraction?

2185. How can ¼ be written as a percent?

2186. How can ¼ be written as a decimal?

2187. What are you finding if you add a series of numbers together and then divide by how many numbers there are: the mode or the average?

2188. What is the average time for a rat to run through a maze if the first rat finished in 12 seconds, the second finished in 8 seconds, and the third finished in 7 seconds? (12 + 8 + 7 = __/3)

2189. What is the average score on the math test if you scored a 90%, Krista scored 80%, and Jimmy scored a 70%? (90 +80 +70 = __/ 3)

2190. What is another name for average: mean or mode?

2191. What is the mean of 2, 3, and 4?

2192. What is the number called that appears most frequently in a series of numbers: mode or mean?

2193. What is the mode in the following numbers: 15, 16, 14, 15, 12, 17, 15, 11, and 15?

2194. What is the name of the middle number in a series of numbers: median or mode?

2195. What should you do first to find the median in a sequence of numbers: place them in order according to their value, add them and divide by the total number?

**2196.** How would you order following sequence of numbers: 5, 3, 7, 9, and 2?

**2197.** What is the median of the number sequence: 2, 3, 5, 7, and 9?

**2198.** What is the mathematical term that refers to the difference between the lowest and the highest values: average or range?

**2199.** What is the range of the sequence: 4, 5, 3, 7, and 9? (9-3)

**2200.** What is the mathematical term for determining the next number in a sequence of numbers: rate of increase or growth pattern?

**2201.** What is the growth pattern of the following sequence: 2, 4, 6, 8, _?

**2202.** What is the growth pattern of the following sequence: 1, 3, 6, 10, _? (+2, +3, etc.)

**2203.** How would you finish the pattern if you multiply by 2 and then add 3: 1, 5, 13, __?

**2204.** Can you read and interpret a line graph, a circle graph, and a bar graph?

**2205.** How many quadrants are in a coordinate graph: 8 or 4?

**2206.** Are the quadrants of a graph always equal?

**2207.** What is the math term that refers to a pictorial representation of relationships or numerical data: a pictograph or a scale?

**2208.** Can you read and interpret a table and a pictograph?

**2209.** What is the math term that represents data on a number line, or other marks that show frequency: line plots or frequency counts?

**2210.** Can you create and interpret line plots?

**2211.** Can you plot data and interpret a frequency chart?

**2212.** What is the name of the graph that has horizontal or vertical rectangles to show the value of different pieces of data: a bar graph or a line graph?

**2213.** What is the name of the graph that shows how information is connected, or how it changes over time: a bar graph or a line graph?

**2214.** What kind of graph would best illustrate the relationship of several parts compared to the whole: a bar graph or a pie chart?

**2215.** What kind of graph or chart would best illustrate the most popular breeds of dogs: a line graph or a pie chart?

**2216.** What kind of graph or chart would best illustrate the number of students that earned an A, B, C, or D on a recent test: a bar graph or a line graph?

**2217.** What kind of graph or chart would best illustrate the change in temperature over a 24 hour period: a bar graph or a line graph?

**2218.** What kind of graph or chart would best illustrate the number of hot dogs that were sold per month at a year-round hot-dog stand: a pie chart or a pictograph?

**2219.** What are you conducting if you tally the number that represents each person's answer: a survey or a questionnaire?

**2220.** What are some topics you might survey your friends about?

**2221.** What is the specific name for the math that involves using letters and symbols to represent numbers that are unknown: geometry or algebra?

**2222.** What are the unknown letters called in algebra: unknowns or variables?

**2223.** What is the answer to the equation: 6 + 2 + 4 ÷3?

**2224.** What is the answer to the following algebraic equation: 6 + b, if b = 3?

**2225.** What is the value of "b" in the following equation: 6 + b = 11?

**2226.** What are the letters called in algebraic expressions?

**2227.** How would you solve for **t** in the following equation: **t** – 15 = 4?

**2228.** How would you solve for **a** in the following: **a** = **b** – 6 and **b** =7? (7-6 = __)

**2229.** Is 4 squared the same as 4 x 4 or 4 x 2?

**2230.** Which multiplication equation is equal to 4 to the third power: 3x3x3 or 4x4x4?

**2231.** What is 2 to the fourth power equal to? (2x2x2x2=_)

**2232.** How would you solve for the exponent **p** if 3 to the "**p**" power = 27?

**2233.** What two measurement systems exist for recording mass, volume, length, and temperature?

**2234.** What is the standard U.S. customary unit for weight?

**2235.** How would you order the following U.S. customary units of weight lightest to heaviest: pound, ton, and ounce?

**2236.** How many ounces are equal to one pound: 16 or 24?

**2237.** Which is more: 33 ounces or 2 pounds?

**2238.** How many pounds are equal to one ton: 1000 or 2000?

**2239.** How many pounds are equal to one half ton?

**2240.** How many pounds equal one quarter ton?

**2241.** Which is less: 3000 pounds or 2 tons?

**2242.** How many inches are equal to one foot?

**2243.** How many feet equal one yard?

**2244.** Which is less: 1 yard or 4 feet?

**2245.** What is the standard unit for mass in the Metric system: gram or liter?

**2246.** How would you put the Metric units of mass in order lightest to heaviest: kilogram, milligram, metric ton, and gram?

**2247.** How many centigrams are equal to one gram: 100 or 1000?

**2248.** Is the weight of a paper clip closer to one gram or one centigram?

**2249.** How many grams are equal to one kilogram: 100 or 1000?

**2250.** Approximately how many pounds are equal to one kilogram: 2 or 3?

**2251.** If an object weighs 2.2 pounds, how many kilograms does it weigh?

**2252.** What is the Metric measurement for volume: liter or pint?

**2253.** How many liters of water equal 1 kilogram: 4 or 1?

**2254.** What are the U.S. customary units in order smallest to largest: foot, yard, inch, and mile?

**2255.** What are the Metric units for length in order smallest to largest: kilometer, meter, millimeter, and centimeter?

**2256.** Which Metric unit is equal to 39.37 inches: one meter or one yard?

**2257.** Which is longer: a meter or a yard?

**2258.** How much is 1/3 of a yard?

**2259.** If one meter measures approximately 39 inches, how much would 1/3 of a meter be?

**2260.** Which Metric unit is equal to 2.5 centimeters: one inch or one foot?

**2261.** Would the diameter of a dime be more like a centimeter or a millimeter?

**2262.** Would the thickness of a dime be more like a centimeter or a millimeter?

**2263.** Which U.S. customary unit is equal to 1760 yards: one kilometer or one mile?

**2264.** Which Metric unit is equal to 0.62 miles: one kilometer or one centimeter?

**2265.** What is the U.S. customary unit for temperature?

**2266.** What is the Metric unit for temperature?

**2267.** If 32 degrees Fahrenheit is the melting point for water, what is the equivalent temperature in Celsius?

**2268.** What temperature is the boiling point for water in degrees Celsius: 100 or 200?

**2269.** If the boiling point is 100 degrees Celsius, what is the equivalent temperature in Fahrenheit: 212 or 112?

**2270.** What is the normal body temperature of a human being in degrees Fahrenheit: 108.6 or 98.6?

**2271.** What are the U.S. customary units for volume in order from smallest to largest: gallon, quart, pint, fluid ounces, and cup?

**2272.** If there are 16 cups in one gallon, how many cups are there in ¼ of a gallon?

**2273.** If there are 4 quarts in a gallon, how many quarts are there in ½ gallon?

**2274.** How many fluid ounces are equal to 1 pint: 8 or 16?

**2275.** If there are 8 fluid ounces in one cup, how many fluid ounces are there in 3 cups?

**2276.** What is a U.S. customary unit that we use to measure the area of farmland: square yards, acres, or square miles?

**2277.** How many pecks are there on one bushel: 2 or 4?

**2278.** What is a U.S. customary unit that we use to measure the quantity of farm produce: peck or bushel?

**2279.** If ¼ bushel or 0.25 is equal to 1 peck, how many pecks are there in 1 full bushel?

**2280.** What is a U.S. customary unit that petroleum is measured in: barrels or drums?

**2281.** What U.S. customary unit are milk and gasoline measured in: Liters or gallons?

**2282.** What is the standard unit of volume in the Metric System?

**2283.** What are the Metric units for volume in order from smallest to largest: kiloliter, milliliter, liter, and centiliter?

**2284.** What is a liter a little more than in U.S. customary units: a quart or a gallon?

**2285.** What is one meter a little more than in U.S. customary units?

**2286.** What is one kilometer a little more than in U.S. customary units?

**2287.** What time is it now?

**2288.** What is the next logical time: 11:00, 11:15, 11:30, _?

**2289.** What are the names of the time zones from west to east: pacific, mountain, central, and _?

**2290.** What is the name of the time zone we live in?

**2291.** Do television shows air at different times depending on the time zone?

**2292.** If you started baking a cake in the oven at 11:10 and you took it out 25 minutes later, what time would it be?

**2293.** If your friend's birthday party begins at 10:30 and ends two and a half hours later, what time do you need to be picked up from the party?

**2294.** What do you say if you are referring to a time before 12:00 noon?

**2295.** What do you say if you are referring to a time after 12:00 noon?

**2296.** What does "ante" translate to in ante-meridiem or AM: before or after?

**2297.** What does "post" translate to in post-meridiem or PM: before or after?

**2298.** What is another way of saying 12:00 at night?

**2299.** How many seconds are there in 1 minute?

**2300.** How many seconds are there in 2 minutes?

**2301.** How many minutes are there in 1 hour?

**2302.** How many minutes are there in 3 hours?

**2303.** How many hours are there in 1 day?

**2304.** How many hours are there in 2 days?

**2305.** How many days is 72 hours?

**2306.** How many hours are in ½ day? (1/2 x 24 = __)

**2307.** How many hours are in ¼ day? (1/4 x 24 = __)

**2308.** How many hours are in ¾ day? (3/4 x 24 = __)

**2309.** How many days are there in 4 weeks?

**2310.** How many weeks are in 3 months?

**2311.** How many months are in ½ year?

**2312.** How many days exactly does it take for the Earth to orbit once around the Sun?

**2313.** How many days are there in one Earth year?

**2314.** How many weeks are there in one year: 48 or 52?

**2315.** How many days are in a Leap year?

**2316.** How do we account for the extra ¼ day that we have every year?

**2317.** What is the month and date of the Leap year day?

**2318.** How many years are there in one decade?

**2319.** How many years are there in one century?

**2320.** How many years would a bicentennial celebration be?

**2321.** Can you read a time line?

**2322.** What is the name of the math that is the study of points, lines, shapes, and angles?

**2323.** What type of tool would be used to draw a simple line or a ray?

**2324.** What is the name of a line that has two points at each end: a line or a line segment?

**2325.** What is the name of the line that has an arrow at each end: a ray or a line?

**2326.** What is the name of the line that has a point at one end and an arrow at the other: ray or line?

**2327.** How is a ray different from a line segment?

**2328.** What are 2 lines called that are the same distance from each other and never cross each other: parallel or perpendicular?

**2329.** What are 2 lines called that form a right angle: parallel or perpendicular?

**2330.** What are 2 lines called that cross each other and form an X: crossing or intersecting?

**2331.** What is it called when there are equal parts or shapes on both sides of a dividing line, or around a figure: intersecting or symmetrical?

**2332.** What is formed when two lines or two line segments meet: an intersection or a right angle?

**2333.** What is the geometric term for the place where two lines come together: the point or the vertex?

**2334.** What is the name of the measuring tool that is used to measure the degrees of angles: compass or protractor?

**2335.** What is the name of the unit of measurement for angles: degrees or coordinates?

**2336.** How many degrees does a full circle measure: 180 or 360?

**2337.** How many degrees does half a circle measure: 180 or 90?

**2338.** How many degrees does one quarter circle measure: 45 or 90?

**2339.** What is the measurement in degrees of a right angle: 90 or 180?

**2340.** Is one quarter of a circle the same as a right angle?

**2341.** If you divided a right angle in half, how many degrees would it measure?

**2342.** What is the name of the angle that has a measurement of less than 90 degrees: acute or obtuse?

**2343.** What is the name of the angle that has a measurement greater than 90 degrees but less than 180 degrees: acute or obtuse?

**2344.** What is the name of an angle that measures exactly 180 degrees: a straight angle or a reflex angle?

**2345.** What is the name of an angle that measures more than 180 degrees: straight or reflex?

**2346.** Are obtuse angles greater than or less than right angles?

**2347.** What is the total measurement in degrees of a triangle: 180 or 360?

**2348.** What is the third measurement of a triangle if one angle measures 80 degrees and a second angle measures 40 degrees?

**2349.** What is the measurement of a straight angle: 90 degrees or 180 degrees?

**2350.** What are plane figures called that have straight sides and are made out of at least three line segments: polygons or octagons?

**2351.** What common plane figures or shapes can you name?

**2352.** How many angles do triangles have?

**2353.** What other words do you know start with the prefix "tri" meaning three?

**2354.** What is the name of a triangle that has three sides each measuring 60 degrees: isosceles, right, or equilateral?

**2355.** What is the name of a triangle that has two sides and two equal angles: isosceles, right, or equilateral?

**2356.** What is the name of a triangle that has no equal sides: isosceles, right, or scalene?

**2357.** What is the name of a triangle that has one right angle: isosceles, right, or equilateral?

**2358.** What is the measurement of each of the two equal angles in a right isosceles triangle if you subtract the 90 degrees of the right angle from 180? (180-90=__/2)

**2359.** What is the term for two triangles that have the same size and shape: equilateral or congruent?

**2360.** What is the name of triangle with three equal sides, each measuring 60 degrees: equilateral or right?

**2361.** What is the geometric term for the longest side of a triangle: the hypotenuse or the Pythagoras?

**2362.** What is the correct formula for finding the area of a triangle: one-half the base times the height, or the length times the width divided by 2?

**2363.** What is a polygon called that has four sides: a quadrilateral or a square?

**2364.** What is the name of the quadrilateral where the opposite sides are the same length: a trapezoid or a rectangle?

**2365.** What is the formula for finding the area of a rectangle: width x height or ½ width x height?

**2366.** What is the formula for finding the area of a square: the length of one side squared or the length of one side times 4?

**2367.** What is the area of a square if you know that one side equals 5 centimeters?

**2368.** What is the name of the quadrilateral that has four equal sides and four right angles?

**2369.** What is the name of the quadrilateral that has one pair of opposite parallel lines: a trapezoid or a parallelogram?

**2370.** What is the name of the quadrilateral where both pairs of the opposite sides are of equal length: a trapezoid or a parallelogram?

**2371.** Would squares, rectangles, and rhombuses be considered parallelograms or trapezoids?

**2372.** What is the name of the quadrilateral where all four sides are of equal length and are parallel: a square or a rectangle?

**2373.** How many diagonal lines does a quadrilateral have: two or four?

**2374.** Can a square be a rectangle, or can a rectangle be a square?

**2375.** What is the name of the polygon that has 5 sides: a pentagon or a hexagon?

**2376.** What is the name of the polygon that has 6 sides: a hexagon or a heptagon?

**2377.** What is the name of the polygon that has 7 sides: a heptagon or a decagon?

**2378.** What is the name of the polygon that has 8 sides: a nonagon or an octagon?

**2379.** What is the name of the polygon that has 9 sides: a nonagon or a pentagon?

**2380.** What is the name of the polygon that has 10 sides: a decagon or a heptagon?

**2381.** What is the formula for finding the area of a shape: width x height, or length squared?

**2382.** What is the area of a rectangle that has sides of 6 feet and 4 feet?

**2383.** What is the name of a flat shape that is round?

**2384.** What is the name of the tool that you use to draw a circle: compass or protractor?

**2385.** How many degrees is a full circle?

**2386.** What is the line segment called that connects two points on a curve: a segment or a chord?

**2387.** What is the line segment called that connects two points through the center of a circle: chord or diameter?

**2388.** What is the length of a chord equal to on a circle: the diameter or the perimeter?

**2389.** What is the measurement of the distance from the center of the circle to any point on the outside of the circle: the perimeter or the radius?

**2390.** What is the measurement of the distance around the edge of a circle: diameter or circumference?

**2391.** What do we multiply the diameter by in order to find the circumference of a circle: the Greek letter pi π, or the length of the chord?

**2392.** Does pi equal the ratio of a circle's circumference to its diameter, or to its perimeter?

**2393.** Does pi equal 3.14 or 2.14?

**2394.** What date in the calendar year do many math students recognize as "pi day?"

**2395.** Which figures have sides, faces, edges, and vertices: planar figures or solid figures?

**2396.** Which figures would have width, depth, and height: planar figures or solid figures?

**2397.** What common solid figures or multi-dimensional shapes can you name?

**2398.** Are solid figures like prisms, cones, spheres, cubes, and cylinders two or three-dimensional?

**2399.** How many rectangles are in a rectangular prism: 3 or 6?

**2400.** Is a cube considered a rectangular prism?

**2401.** What is the formula for measuring the volume or cubic units of a rectangular prism: length x width, or length x width x height?

**2402.** If a rectangular prism measures 4 inches long, 2 inches wide, and 3 inches tall, what is its volume in cubic inches?

**2403.** What is the word "Math" short for?

**2404.** What is the term for the most elementary form of mathematics?

**2405.** What is your favorite type of math?

# APPENDIX – Answers to Questions

## Math Answers

### Pre-School

1. Counts to 10
2. 9
3. 6
4. 7
5. Counts past 6
6. Counts backward from 8
7. 6
8. IIII with slash for five
9. Ten Little Indians, etc.
10. Prime numbers
11. The sum
12. The difference
13. Can complete puzzle
14. States empty or full
15. 10
16. A city
17. A state
18. 2
19. Equal
20. The same
21. Equal
22. Equals
23. Names large objects
24. Names small objects
25. Names blue objects
26. Names square objects
27. Round
28. Can name round objects
29. A rectangle
30. Can name rectangular objects
31. Square
32. Yes
33. Ice cube, pizza box, dice, etc.
34. A diamond
35. Yes
36. Yes
37. Both
38. White
39. White, blue
40. Piano, scissors
41. Recites phone number
42. Recites address numbers
43. Names objects inside
44. Names objects outside
45. Names objects above
46. Names objects below
47. Names objects on bed
48. Names objects under bed
49. The right
50. States correct hand
51. Long
52. Short
53. Light
54. Heavy
55. A bowl
56. Wide
57. Narrow
58. A penny
59. A nickel
60. A dime
61. A quarter

### Math – Kindergarten

62. Counts to 100
63. Counts to 100 by 5's
64. Counts to 100 by 10's
65. Zero
66. Counts forward from 7
67. Counts backward from 20
68. 20
69. Names blue objects
70. 8
71. 2
72. 80
73. 6
74. Round, circle
75. One half
76. Yes
77. In half
78. Yes
79. Yes
80. Teaspoons
81. A tablespoon
82. Measuring spoons
83. A triangle
84. Square
85. A rectangle
86. Names round objects
87. Names square objects
88. 4
89. Names triangular objects
90. 3
91. Names rectangular objects
92. 4
93. An egg, rug, a racetrack, etc.
94. 10
95. 5
96. Says correct number
97. Indicates age with fingers
98. Holds up 2 fingers
99. Holds up 2 fingers
100. Counts backward from 10
101. Counts to 20 by 2's
102. Yes
103. Counts to 20 by 5's
104. 14
105. 5
106. 0
107. 2
108. 4
109. 10
110. Yes
111. A plus
112. A dash
113. 2
114. 5
115. 3
116. 2 dashes
117. One cent
118. Five cents
119. Ten cents
120. 25 cents
121. Copper
122. One line
123. Two lines

124. 4
125. A nickel
126. A dime
127. A quarter
128. Yes
129. Yes
130. Yes
131. Yes
132. Different sizes
133. Dime
134. A 50 cent piece
135. 0, it is round
136. Heads
137. Tails
138. C with line through it
139. The dollar
140. An S with two lines
141. Names red objects
142. Sorts clothes by color
143. Four lines with a fifth slash
144. Names big toys
145. Names small toys
146. Names inside objects
147. Names outside objects
148. Identifies objects on left
149. Identifies objects on right
150. Identifies objects in middle
151. On top

152. Head
153. Legs
154. Estimates number of animals
155. Blue
156. Green, pink
157. Turtles, cats
158. A clock, watch, or phone
159. 12
160. Yes
161. 3:00
162. A ruler or yardstick
163. Names long animals
164. Names short animals
165. A yardstick
166. A thermometer
167. A calculator
168. A scale
169. Names heavy animals
170. Names light animals
171. Names heavy objects
172. Names light objects
173. The afternoon
174. States when breakfast was eaten
175. After
176. A. M.
177. States time of day
178. A calendar

179. Says days of week in order
180. 7
181. 30 or 31, except February
182. Different
183. Tuesday
184. Wednesday
185. Sunday
186. Winter
187. Winter
188. States empty or full
189. Half-full
190. Names paired items
191. Puts right hand on head
192. Puts left hand between knees
193. Puts right hand under left foot
194. Puts left hand beside right knee
195. The blue section
196. A submarine sandwich
197. A ruler
198. A skyscraper
199. A dog
200. A cup
201. A frog
202. An elephant
203. A beach ball

# Math – 1<sup>st</sup> Grade

204. Counts to 100 by 5's
205. Counts to 100 by 10's
206. Counts to 50 by 2's
207. Counts back from 10
208. 17
209. 50
210. 1
211. By 5's
212. Pairs or twins
213. Socks, shoes, gloves, boots, etc.
214. Pants, sunglasses, scissors
215. Zero
216. States math games
217. Yes
218. First
219. Second
220. Third
221. Tenth
222. Seventh
223. States weather
224. Can read thermometer
225. Temperature
226. Rain gauge, barometer, satellite

227. Yes
228. A plane, kite, bird, etc.
229. Wind
230. Energy
231. Once
232. Twice
233. 4
234. 20
235. 8
236. 35
237. Even
238. 7
239. 10
240. Odd
241. Odd
242. 31
243. 49
244. 29
245. 4 cups
246. Eyes, ears, etc.
247. Estimates animal total
248. 4
249. 3
250. 4
251. A circle

252. Names round objects
253. Names rectangular objects
254. Names square objects
255. Square
256. Oval
257. Cube
258. Sphere
259. A solid shape
260. Solid shapes
261. Simple shapes
262. An ice cream cone, party hat, etc.
263. Open shape
264. Closed shape
265. Names straight objects
266. Names curved objects
267. A triangle, arc, etc.
268. A rainbow
269. A sandwich, an hour, etc.
270. Yellow, blue
271. Yes
272. 70
273. 49
274. All of them
275. Greater than

| | | | | | |
|---|---|---|---|---|---|
| 276. | 20 is less than 30 | 336. | 14 | 394. | A plus sign |
| 277. | They are equal | 337. | 21 | 395. | 5 |
| 278. | Equal | 338. | 59 | 396. | 2+3=5 |
| 279. | 1 | 339. | Less than | 397. | Subtraction |
| 280. | 2 | 340. | Equal | 398. | A minus |
| 281. | 4 | 341. | Less | 399. | 1 |
| 282. | 6 | 342. | Greater than | 400. | 4-3=1 |
| 283. | 8 | 343. | Greater than | 401. | 12 |
| 284. | 10 | 344. | Less than | 402. | One foot |
| 285. | 12 | 345. | Equal to | 403. | A yardstick |
| 286. | 14 | 346. | Greater than | 404. | Equal to |
| 287. | 16 | 347. | 10 | 405. | Yes |
| 288. | 18 | 348. | Right | 406. | Inches, feet, yard |
| 289. | 20 | 349. | Most | 407. | 12 inches |
| 290. | 30 | 350. | Gets taller; bigger | 408. | The mile |
| 291. | 40 | 351. | Gets colder; warmer; etc. | 409. | A scale |
| 292. | 50 | 352. | Increases | 410. | The pound |
| 293. | 60 | 353. | 3 | 411. | 17 ounces |
| 294. | 70 | 354. | 12, 22, 42 | 412. | States weight |
| 295. | 80 | 355. | 42, 22, 12 | 413. | States length using hands |
| 296. | 90 | 356. | 7 | 414. | A thermometer |
| 297. | 100 | 357. | 5 | 415. | Fahrenheit |
| 298. | 18 | 358. | 6 | 416. | Yes |
| 299. | 21 | 359. | 4 tens and 9 ones | 417. | Millimeter, centimeter, meter |
| 300. | 24 | 360. | Estimates number | | |
| 301. | Yes | 361. | Estimates time | 418. | 18 centimeters |
| 302. | Yes | 362. | A calendar | 419. | Celsius |
| 303. | Yes | 363. | Yes | 420. | The kilometer |
| 304. | Equal to | 364. | 12 | 421. | Grams |
| 305. | Yes | 365. | 30 | 422. | 13 grams |
| 306. | 10 dogs | 366. | 7 | 423. | One thousand |
| 307. | 6 pieces | 367. | Thursday | 424. | Liters |
| 308. | 11 | 368. | Monday | 425. | Names hot objects |
| 309. | 4 | 369. | Friday | 426. | Names cold objects |
| 310. | A dash | 370. | Wednesday | 427. | Full |
| 311. | 4 | 371. | Saturday | 428. | Empty |
| 312. | 9 | 372. | Friday and Saturday | 429. | Yes |
| 313. | 3 | 373. | 60 | 430. | Names solids |
| 314. | 10 | 374. | 60 | 431. | Names liquids |
| 315. | 20 etc. | 375. | 24 | 432. | A pint |
| 316. | 19 etc. | 376. | 9:30 | 433. | A quart |
| 317. | 80 etc. | 377. | States type of clock | 434. | A gallon |
| 318. | 20 | 378. | The p.m. | 435. | Cup, pint, quart, gallon |
| 319. | 22 | 379. | a.m. | 436. | Liquid capacity |
| 320. | 11 | 380. | 3 hours | 437. | One half pint |
| 321. | 9 | 381. | 12 | 438. | The gallon |
| 322. | 4 | 382. | The first | 439. | Gas, milk, water, etc. |
| 323. | 8-4 | 383. | December | 440. | 2 cups |
| 324. | 2+7 | 384. | Last | 441. | 4 cups |
| 325. | 2: 1-1 | 385. | February (etc.) | 442. | 2 pints |
| 326. | 8,7,6,5,4,3,2,1,0 | 386. | States grade | 443. | 4 quarts |
| 327. | 7 | 387. | States grade | 444. | 7 cups |
| 328. | 30 | 388. | States grade | 445. | Gallons |
| 329. | 90 | 389. | December, January, and February | 446. | Liter |
| 330. | 9 | | | 447. | Full |
| 331. | 6-2=4 | 390. | June, July, and August | 448. | Half-full |
| 332. | Plus sign | 391. | September, October, and November | 449. | Driving to school |
| 333. | Minus sign | | | 450. | Eating grapes |
| 334. | The difference | 392. | March, April, and May | 451. | The white bag |
| 335. | 11-6 | 393. | Addition | 452. | The red bag |

453. Equal
454. 4
455. Yes
456. A part
457. Numerator
458. Denominator
459. One-half
460. One-third
461. 4
462. 4
463. 3
464. A circle
465. 6
466. 8
467. 8
468. Stop sign
469. A skirt
470. A sphere
471. A cylinder
472. A cone
473. A cube
474. A triangle
475. An open shape
476. Closed shape
477. Yes

478. Symmetrical
479. Diagonally
480. The bar graph with 40
481. Tally marks
482. 2
483. 3
484. 1
485. A nickel
486. A dime
487. A quarter
488. Yes
489. Yes, can add coins
490. 2
491. 2 dimes and 1 nickel
492. 41 cents
493. 35 cents
494. 65 cents
495. 78 cents
496. One dollar
497. One quarter
498. 50 cents or half a dollar
499. A quarter
500. A quarter
501. 60 cents
502. 4

503. 2
504. 4
505. One dollar
506. No
507. No
508. Two
509. More than two
510. Certain
511. Impossible
512. Unlikely
513. Unlikely
514. Letter I
515. Letter V
516. Letter X
517. Letter L
518. 15
519. 30
520. 14
521. 68
522. 5
523. $1 + 4 = 5$
524. Yes
525. 4
526. The mode
527. 6

## Math – 2$^{nd}$ Grade

528. Counts to 100
529. Counts to 100 by 20's
530. Counts to 100 by 2's
531. Counts to 100 by 5's
532. Counts to 1000 by 100's
533. Counts upwards from 600
534. 980
535. No
536. Counts back from 100
537. 25, 33, 44
538. 55
539. 98
540. Counts by 2's from 26
541. Blue fish
542. Blue, yellow, yellow
543. Odd
544. Even
545. 2
546. 1
547. 8
548. Names ordinals
549. States grade
550. 1$^{st}$
551. 2$^{nd}$
552. 3$^{rd}$
553. 4$^{th}$
554. 5$^{th}$
555. 6$^{th}$
556. 7$^{th}$
557. 8$^{th}$

558. 9$^{th}$
559. 10$^{th}$
560. 50$^{th}$
561. 50$^{th}$ and 75$^{th}$
562. 39$^{th}$
563. 245
564. The sum
565. The difference
566. Minus
567. Plus
568. 18
569. 17
570. 25
571. 80
572. 29
573. 24
574. 86
575. 51
576. 500
577. 250
578. 16
579. 44
580. $3 + 12 = 15$
581. $8 + 12 = 20$
582. 10
583. 9
584. 6
585. 18
586. 13 lions
587. 36 cookies

588. $200 + 150 = 350$
589. 40
590. 50
591. 8
592. 5
593. $2 + 7$
594. 9
595. 5
596. 0
597. $8 - 0$
598. 30
599. 63
600. 14
601. 13
602. 40
603. 300
604. 700
605. 200
606. Ten
607. $12 + 2 = 14$
608. 12-2
609. States equation that equals 10
610. 10
611. $20 - 5 = 15$
612. $30 - 20 = 10$
613. 6 peas
614. 14 Legos
615. $4 - 2 = 2$
616. $40 - 20 = 20$

| | | | | | | | |
|---|---|---|---|---|---|---|---|
| **617.** | 9 leaves | **677.** | 6 | **737.** | 9:00 |
| **618.** | 6 | **678.** | 15 | **738.** | 2:45 |
| **619.** | 20 | **679.** | That number | **739.** | 2:30 |
| **620.** | 5 | **680.** | Zero | **740.** | 7:15 |
| **621.** | 74 – 4 | **681.** | Zero | **741.** | Quarter to nine |
| **622.** | 46 | **682.** | 25 | **742.** | Yes |
| **623.** | 10 | **683.** | 24 | **743.** | Yes |
| **624.** | Yes | **684.** | 12 | **744.** | Names time zone |
| **625.** | 4 | **685.** | 25 | **745.** | p.m. |
| **626.** | 55 | **686.** | 45 | **746.** | a.m. |
| **627.** | 2 | **687.** | 2 | **747.** | 2:00 |
| **628.** | 10 + 2 (Etc.) | **688.** | 2 | **748.** | 6 hours |
| **629.** | 7 + 5 = 12 | **689.** | 5 | **749.** | 35 degrees |
| **630.** | No | **690.** | 4 | **750.** | States height |
| **631.** | + 10 | **691.** | 6 | **751.** | States weight |
| **632.** | Sweatshirts | **692.** | Yes | **752.** | 16 |
| **633.** | Reads a pictograph | **693.** | Yes | **753.** | 2,000 |
| **634.** | Reads a line graph | **694.** | Yes | **754.** | 3,000 |
| **635.** | The middle | **695.** | Yes | **755.** | Truck, monument, etc. |
| **636.** | Less than | **696.** | Top | **756.** | A gram |
| **637.** | Greater than | **697.** | Bottom | **757.** | 16 ounces |
| **638.** | Equal to | **698.** | One over four | **758.** | 2 grams |
| **639.** | 76 | **699.** | One over two | **759.** | 4 Kilograms |
| **640.** | 49 | **700.** | One over three | **760.** | Estimates dresser height |
| **641.** | Greater than | **701.** | ½ | **761.** | Estimates dresser length |
| **642.** | Equal to | **702.** | 6/7, 6/8, 6/9 | **762.** | A meter |
| **643.** | 2 and 6 | **703.** | Red | **763.** | Millimeter, centimeter, kilometer |
| **644.** | 1 and 5 | **704.** | Yes | | |
| **645.** | 26, 28 etc. | **705.** | ½ | **764.** | 12 |
| **646.** | 35, 37, etc., | **706.** | 2/3 | **765.** | 3 |
| **647.** | 70, 71, 77 | **707.** | ¾ | **766.** | Estimates length of shoe |
| **648.** | 99, 92, 88 | **708.** | ½ | **767.** | 12 inches |
| **649.** | 4 | **709.** | Yes | **768.** | 11 feet long |
| **650.** | 0 | **710.** | 1/7 | **769.** | 25 centimeters |
| **651.** | 1 | **711.** | 2/3 | **770.** | Estimates distance |
| **652.** | Tens | **712.** | ½ cup, etc. | **771.** | A kilometer |
| **653.** | Tens | **713.** | Rounded up | **772.** | One kilometer |
| **654.** | 9 tens and 5 ones | **714.** | 10 | **773.** | Estimates miles |
| **655.** | 3, 4, 5 | **715.** | 90 | **774.** | Inch, foot, yard |
| **656.** | 3, 0, 4, 2 | **716.** | 30 | **775.** | A meter stick |
| **657.** | 1 | **717.** | 30 | **776.** | Cup, pint, quart, gallon |
| **658.** | Yes | **718.** | 30 | **777.** | A liter |
| **659.** | 7 | **719.** | 80 | **778.** | 2 liters |
| **660.** | Hundreds | **720.** | 170 | **779.** | 2,000 milliliters |
| **661.** | Thousands | **721.** | 8,000 | **780.** | 12 fluid ounces |
| **662.** | 4 tens and 2 ones | **722.** | 71 | **781.** | 4 cups |
| **663.** | 8 | **723.** | $3.00 | **782.** | 2 cups |
| **664.** | 5 tens and 15 ones | **724.** | 90 degrees | **783.** | Cups |
| **665.** | Yes | **725.** | Yes, can tell time | **784.** | A stopwatch |
| **666.** | 5 | **726.** | States the correct time | **785.** | Temperature |
| **667.** | 329 | **727.** | 60 | **786.** | Length |
| **668.** | 7,384 | **728.** | 60 | **787.** | Weight |
| **669.** | A decimal point | **729.** | 24 | **788.** | Baking powder, salt, etc. |
| **670.** | Yes | **730.** | 7 | **789.** | Flour, sugar, etc. |
| **671.** | One fourth | **731.** | 4 | **790.** | Says date |
| **672.** | One and three fourths | **732.** | 12 | **791.** | October |
| **673.** | 2:1 | **733.** | 365 ¼ | **792.** | July |
| **674.** | 4:1 | **734.** | 30 | **793.** | 31 |
| **675.** | The product | **735.** | Week | **794.** | 31 |
| **676.** | 6 | **736.** | 2:00 | **795.** | 28 |

796. 29
797. September 1
798. April 30ᵗʰ
799. January 1
800. The year
801. A leap year
802. States today's day
803. States day before yesterday
804. Friday
805. Saturday
806. Sunday
807. Yes
808. December, January, February
809. April, May, June
810. June, July, August
811. September, October, November
812. Autumn/fall
813. Summer
814. States dates of holidays
815. Yes
816. States house number
817. States phone number
818. Yes
819. Yes
820. Names other currency
821. No
822. The pound
823. A quarter
824. A dime
825. A nickel
826. A penny
827. 25

828. 4
829. One fourth
830. 10
831. 5
832. 2 dimes and 1 nickel, etc.
833. 2 dimes and 1 nickel, etc.
834. 6 dimes and 3 nickels
835. 15 cents
836. 100
837. 25
838. 2
839. 5
840. 40 cents
841. Yes
842. One half dollar
843. 2
844. 2
845. 50 cents
846. 41 cents
847. 38 cents
848. 90 cents
849. 2 dimes and 1 nickel
850. 1 quarter and 1 nickel
851. 1 quarter, 2 dimes, 1 penny
852. No
853. Yes
854. No
855. 20 cents
856. Yes
857. 25 cents
858. 6 dollars
859. 45 dollars
860. Yes
861. Former presidents

862. Yes
863. Diagonal slash
864. On a diagonal
865. Horizontal
866. Vertical
867. Bar graph
868. Higher
869. Yes
870. Basketball
871. Soccer
872. Geometric
873. Sun, moon, ball, etc.
874. Yard, football field, table, etc.
875. Pyramid, tent, pizza, etc.
876. Serving plate, stone, racetrack, etc.
877. Earth, globe, ball, etc.
878. Tepee, evergreen tree, road markers, etc.
879. Candle, flashlight, beaker, etc.
880. Add
881. 20 cm
882. 15 feet
883. 32 feet
884. Base times itself
885. 16
886. 9
887. Unlikely
888. Subtract the lowest from highest
889. 9
890. Mode
891. 5

## Math – 3ʳᵈ Grade

892. Zero
893. Infinity
894. Counts to 1000
895. Skip-counts to 1000
896. Yes
897. Writes 10
898. Writes 56
899. Writes 414
900. Writes 100
901. Writes 1000
902. Writes 10,000
903. Writes 100,000
904. 100
905. 1,000
906. 10,000
907. 100,000
908. 3,000
909. 54,100
910. 235,000
911. 9,999

912. 57
913. 180
914. The thousands
915. 6 thousands, 2 hundreds, 9 tens, and 5 ones
916. The thousands
917. The hundreds
918. The tens
919. The ones
920. 2
921. 5
922. 8
923. 9
924. 60
925. Eight thousand three hundred twenty nine
926. Forty six thousand eight hundred seventeen
927. Twenty eight thousand five hundred forty two

928. 500 tens
929. 30 hundreds
930. 476
931. 300 + 20 + 5
932. 70, 700, 7,000
933. 150
934. 100
935. Adds 2 three digit numbers
936. 333
937. Even
938. 18
939. Add 10
940. 35, 55, 65
941. Greater than
942. Greater than
943. Equal to
944. Less than
945. Adds numbers 3 or more digits

946. Subtracts numbers 3 or more digits
947. 300
948. $30 + 7 = 37$
949. Yes
950. Round up
951. 70
952. 30
953. 10
954. 100
955. 100
956. 400
957. 300
958. 600
959. 7,000
960. 439,000
961. 80,000
962. 200,000
963. 8 dollars
964. 50 dollars
965. $70 + 30 = 100$
966. $50 - 20 = 30$
967. Yes
968. $50 - 20 = 30$
969. $30 + 50 = 80$
970. $30 \times 4 = 120$
971. 10
972. Arabic
973. Roman numerals
974. One
975. Five
976. Ten
977. Fifty
978. One hundred
979. Five hundred
980. One thousand
981. To the right
982. To the left
983. Add them
984. Subtract them
985. $5 - 1 = 4$
986. Two
987. Fifteen
988. Thirty
989. Four
990. Nine
991. Fourteen
992. 36
993. Yes
994. 1980
995. 1,500
996. CCV
997. Cites all ordinals to tenth
998. States date with ordinal
999. Fourteenth
1000. $50^{th}$
1001. Yes
1002. A positive
1003. A negative
1004. A negative number

1005. A negative number
1006. A negative number
1007. A positive number
1008. Division
1009. Times
1010. X
1011. Yes
1012. Yes
1013. The Factors
1014. 25
1015. Yes
1016. Yes
1017. Multiplication table
1018. 0
1019. 1 (2,3,4,5,6,7,8,9)
1020. 2 (4,6,8,19,12,14,18)
1021. 3 (6,9,12,15,18,21,24,27)
1022. 4 (8,12,16,20,24,28,32,36)
1023. 5 (10,15,20,25,30,35,40,45)
1024. 6 (12,18,24,30,36,42,48,54)
1025. 7 (14,21,28,35,42,49,56,63)
1026. 8 (16,24,32,40,48,56,64,72)
1027. 9 (18,27,36,45,54,63,72,81)
1028. 10 (20,30,40,50,60,70,80, 90)
1029. 5
1030. 100
1031. 1,000
1032. Two
1033. 600
1034. 10,000
1035. 666
1036. 30
1037. First
1038. The distributive
1039. 50
1040. 14
1041. The associative
1042. 4
1043. The commutative
1044. $3 \times 2$
1045. The identity property
1046. 0
1047. 1
1048. The identity property
1049. The associative
1050. The commutative
1051. The distributive
1052. A square number
1053. Yes
1054. 9
1055. Yes
1056. 25
1057. 16
1058. 49
1059. 100
1060. Yes
1061. 5
1062. 4
1063. 7

1064. 10
1065. 36
1066. Multiplies 3 or more numbers
1067. 100, $8 \times 10 = 80$, + 6
1068. 24 points
1069. Division
1070. 3
1071. 3
1072. Line with a dot above and below it
1073. 2
1074. The dividend
1075. The divisor
1076. 0
1077. 7 (that number)
1078. 1 (2,3,4,5,6,7,8,9,10)
1079. 1 (2,3,4,5,6,7,8,9,10)
1080. 1 (2,3,4,5,6,7,8,9,10)
1081. 1 (2,3,4,5,6,7,8,9,10)
1082. 1 (2,3,4,5,6,7,8,9,10)
1083. 1 (2,3,4,5,6,7,8,9,10)
1084. 1 (2,3,4,5,6,7,8,9,10)
1085. 1 (2,3,4,5,6,7,8,9,10)
1086. 1 (2,3,4,5,6,7,8,9,10)
1087. 1 (2,3,4,5,6,7,8,9,10)
1088. 1 (2,3,4,5,6,7,8,9,10)
1089. 6
1090. An inverse operation
1091. $6 \times 7 = 42$
1092. 4+4+4+4
1093. $15 + 5 = 20$
1094. $6 \times 2 = 12$
1095. 50
1096. 100
1097. 70
1098. 80
1099. 40
1100. 90
1101. Yes (1,210)
1102. No
1103. Yes (25)
1104. No
1105. Yes (24)
1106. No
1107. The remainder
1108. Yes
1109. Remainder 1
1110. 7 and remainder 2
1111. Input/Output Table
1112. Rule: Divide by 2
1113. Yes
1114. Multiply
1115. 12 (3x4)
1116. The variable
1117. b
1118. 12
1119. Yes
1120. $28 \div 2$
1121. 1,10,100,1,000

1122. 3
1123. 24 ÷ 8 = 3
1124. Fractions
1125. ¾ and ¼
1126. Numerator
1127. Denominator
1128. Yes
1129. 1
1130. Whole numbers
1131. A mixed number
1132. 1 and 2
1133. 3
1134. 3
1135. Yes
1136. 6
1137. Yes
1138. ½
1139. ½
1140. ¾
1141. ½
1142. Yes
1143. 1
1144. ¾
1145. 3/8
1146. Greater than
1147. 5/8
1148. ¾
1149. Divide
1150. 18 ÷ 3 = 6
1151. Yes
1152. 2.4
1153. ¼
1154. ½
1155. ¾
1156. Yes
1157. 8/100
1158. 2/25
1159. 2/3
1160. 9.81
1161. 4.03
1162. 3.4, 3.5, 3.6
1163. 5.6
1164. 1.2
1165. 3.6
1166. .25
1167. .75
1168. .50
1169. Can read graphs
1170. Can find coordinates
1171. Can graph points
1172. Can interpret line graphs
1173. Can create pictographs
1174. Can interpret Venn diagram
1175. In the middle
1176. States money amount
1177. $1, $5, $10, $20
1178. Currency
1179. Yes
1180. No

1181. States coins with values
1182. $23
1183. 89 cents
1184. $6.50
1185. No
1186. $16
1187. $7.25
1188. $8
1189. Thermometer
1190. Celsius
1191. Fahrenheit
1192. 45 degrees
1193. 32
1194. Water
1195. Hot
1196. Cold
1197. Miles
1198. One mile
1199. Yards
1200. Ruler
1201. 12
1202. 3
1203. 36
1204. Feet
1205. Ruler, measuring tape, level, etc.
1206. Can estimate length
1207. A scale
1208. Lb.
1209. Oz.
1210. 16
1211. Yes
1212. Cup, pint, quart, gallon
1213. 2
1214. 2
1215. 4
1216. One gallon
1217. 8
1218. 10 pints
1219. Millimeter, centimeter, meter, kilometer
1220. Grams
1221. One kilogram
1222. 1,000 grams
1223. Ball is heavier
1224. The liter
1225. States time
1226. 60
1227. 60
1228. 180
1229. 24
1230. A.M.
1231. P.M.
1232. 7:45
1233. 3:40
1234. 4:20
1235. 6:55
1236. Noon
1237. Midnight
1238. Twenty to four

1239. Big hand on 2, little on 7
1240. 5:15
1241. 25 minutes
1242. Can read time schedule
1243. Can read a timeline
1244. Historical events, etc.
1245. Says today's date
1246. March 4th
1247. July 31st
1248. States dates with numbers
1249. States birthdate with numbers
1250. States day of week
1251. Sunday
1252. 7
1253. 4
1254. 365 ¼
1255. February
1256. Every 4 years
1257. 10
1258. 100
1259. 1000
1260. Geometry
1261. "Gee, I'm a Tree"
1262. Yes
1263. Names geometric shapes
1264. Polygons
1265. No
1266. Yes
1267. Line segments
1268. Horizontal
1269. Vertical
1270. Perpendicular
1271. Parallel
1272. 4
1273. Picture, table, dice, etc.
1274. 4
1275. Football field, table, etc.
1276. Yes
1277. 3
1278. Pizza, piece of pie, etc.
1279. Equilateral
1280. Isosceles
1281. Four
1282. Five
1283. Six
1284. Seven
1285. Eight
1286. An octagon
1287. A line
1288. A line segment
1289. A ray
1290. A vertex
1291. Letters
1292. Both
1293. Yes
1294. Angles
1295. An angle
1296. A right angle
1297. 4

1298. Symmetrical
1299. Congruent
1300. Line of symmetry
1301. 1
1302. Infinite
1303. Yes
1304. Reflected
1305. Rotated
1306. Translated
1307. Perimeter
1308. Add
1309. 12

1310. 9
1311. 20
1312. 18
1313. 4
1314. Area
1315. Yes
1316. Multiply
1317. 18
1318. 25
1319. Solids
1320. Solids
1321. Its base

1322. A pyramid
1323. A face
1324. An edge
1325. The face
1326. A vertex
1327. Multiply
1328. 40
1329. States favorite area
1330. Explains practicality of math

# Math – 4<sup>th</sup> Grade

1331. Tens
1332. 1
1333. Hundreds
1334. 2
1335. One thousand
1336. 3
1337. Ten thousand
1338. 4
1339. One hundred thousand
1340. 5
1341. One million
1342. 6
1343. Ten million
1344. One hundred million
1345. One billion
1346. One trillion
1347. Stars, National Debt, etc.
1348. A comma
1349. 3
1350. One million, four hundred thirty four thousand, five hundred and sixty seven.
1351. No
1352. Yes
1353. 3
1354. 5
1355. 6
1356. 4
1357. Ten
1358. A decade
1359. A century
1360. 100,500
1361. Eight thousand, two hundred and forty three
1362. 5,040
1363. Positive
1364. Negative
1365. Even
1366. Odd
1367. Yes
1368. Yes

1369. Arabic
1370. I,II, III, IV, and V
1371. VI, VII, VIII,IX, and X
1372. 50
1373. 100
1374. 500
1375. 1,000
1376. Subtract
1377. 40
1378. Add
1379. 60
1380. 1150
1381. 18
1382. MMXV
1383. Yes
1384. Down
1385. Round up
1386. 3,000
1387. 2,000
1388. 2,900
1389. 2,260
1390. A prime number
1391. A composite number
1392. A prime number
1393. No
1394. Prime numbers
1395. Composite numbers
1396. Composite number
1397. Prime number
1398. Yes
1399. 140,000
1400. One million
1401. 6,352
1402. The associative
1403. The commutative
1404. The identity
1405. 8,000
1406. Yes
1407. Yes
1408. 101,000
1409. 165,000
1410. 350,000

1411. 500
1412. Yes
1413. 3 and 8
1414. 24
1415. 4, 6, 8, 10, etc.
1416. 12, 18, 24, 30, etc.
1417. 7
1418. 9
1419. 6 and 9
1420. 12
1421. A square
1422. Yes
1423. 4
1424. 25
1425. 36
1426. 49
1427. 56
1428. 81
1429. 100
1430. 2
1431. 6
1432. 5
1433. 9
1434. 7
1435. 11
1436. 8
1437. 12
1438. 24
1439. 0
1440. 440
1441. 2200
1442. Yes
1443. Add them
1444. 4
1445. 80,000
1446. The identity
1447. The distributive
1448. The associative
1449. The zero property of multiplication
1450. Identity property
1451. 12,000

1452. 70,000
1453. Greater than
1454. Equal to
1455. Less than
1456. Division
1457. 20 ÷ 2 = 10
1458. 3 x 8 = 24
1459. 20
1460. 5
1461. 4
1462. 9
1463. The dividend
1464. The quotient
1465. The divisor
1466. 20
1467. Yes
1468. That number
1469. 1
1470. 12/3
1471. 4
1472. A factor
1473. 1,2, and 4
1474. 1,2,3,4,6,8,12, and 24
1475. 1,2, and 4
1476. 2 Remainder 1
1477. 4 Remainder 2
1478. 132
1479. 82
1480. 321
1481. 8 x 3 = 24
1482. 90
1483. 60
1484. 8 Remainder 3
1485. Less than
1486. Greater than
1487. Greater than
1488. Yes
1489. Algebra
1490. 20
1491. 7
1492. 6
1493. Yes
1494. Yes
1495. 24
1496. 4
1497. 15
1498. Dollar
1499. Euro, Pound, Yen, etc.
1500. Letter "S" with two lines through it
1501. Letter "C" with line through it
1502. $1.25
1503. A fifty dollar bill
1504. $490
1505. $500
1506. $30
1507. Yes (No)
1508. 85 cents
1509. $45

1510. $7
1511. $5.50
1512. $8.00
1513. $4.80
1514. $4.00
1515. George Washington
1516. Abraham Lincoln
1517. Alexander Hamilton
1518. Andrew Jackson
1519. Ulysses S. Grant
1520. Abraham Lincoln
1521. Thomas Jefferson
1522. Franklin D. Roosevelt
1523. George Washington
1524. Seconds, minutes, hours, days, weeks, months, year
1525. 365 ¼
1526. Add one day, February 29th, every four years
1527. 182 ½
1528. 24 hours
1529. 12 hours
1530. 6 hours
1531. 18 hours
1532. 60 seconds
1533. 60 minutes
1534. 1 ½ hours
1535. 30 minutes
1536. 15 minutes
1537. 75 minutes
1538. 192 minutes
1539. 2 minutes, four seconds
1540. 135 minutes
1541. 21 days
1542. Time zones
1543. Names time zone
1544. Yes
1545. 9:25
1546. Twenty minutes to ten
1547. 2:25
1548. 6:30
1549. Yes
1550. U.S. customary units
1551. Inches, feet, yards, miles
1552. 12
1553. ½, ¼, 1/16, 1/8, etc.
1554. Estimate
1555. 3 feet
1556. 4 feet
1557. 36
1558. 18
1559. A mile
1560. 2,640
1561. A mile
1562. 6 feet
1563. Ounces, pounds, tons
1564. 16
1565. 8
1566. 12
1567. 32

1568. Pounds
1569. 3 pounds
1570. Oz.
1571. Lb.
1572. 2000 pounds
1573. 3 tons
1574. T
1575. 7 tons
1576. Cup, pint, quart, gallon
1577. Teaspoon, tablespoon, cup, stick (of butter)
1578. 3
1579. tsp.
1580. Tbsp.
1581. 8 fluid ounces
1582. C.
1583. ½, 1/3, ¼, 1 cup
1584. 8
1585. 2
1586. Pt.
1587. 2
1588. Qt.
1589. 4
1590. 3 pints
1591. 3 and 1/3
1592. Metric
1593. Decimal
1594. 10
1595. 100
1596. 1000
1597. 10
1598. 3.2
1599. cm.
1600. mm.
1601. 100
1602. M.
1603. A meter
1604. 1000
1605. km.
1606. A kilometer
1607. 62
1608. Liter
1609. 100
1610. 1000
1611. cl.
1612. l.
1613. 500
1614. Milligram, gram, kilogram, metric ton
1615. 1000
1616. 10
1617. mg.
1618. cg.
1619. 1000
1620. g.
1621. 100
1622. kg.
1623. Metric system
1624. Celsius
1625. Fahrenheit

| | | |
|---|---|---|
| 1626. 0 | 1686. ½ | 1746. Perpendicular |
| 1627. Freezes | 1687. ¾ | 1747. Parallel |
| 1628. Fractions | 1688. With decimals | 1748. Horizontal |
| 1629. 2 | 1689. $6.75 | 1749. Vertical |
| 1630. 10 | 1690. $1.25 | 1750. Diagonal |
| 1631. ½ | 1691. 10 | 1751. A polygon |
| 1632. ¼ | 1692. A decade | 1752. A triangle |
| 1633. Yes | 1693. Two point five zero | 1753. A quadrilateral |
| 1634. 6/8, 9/16, etc. | 1694. .1 | 1754. A square and a rectangle |
| 1635. 2/6, 3/9, etc. | 1695. .01 | 1755. A parallelogram |
| 1636. 3/5 | 1696. .001 | 1756. A trapezoid |
| 1637. 4/8 | 1697. Equal to | 1757. A square |
| 1638. Improper fraction | 1698. Yes | 1758. A rhombus |
| 1639. 1 | 1699. Greater than | 1759. A quadrilateral |
| 1640. Improper | 1700. 2.4 | 1760. A pentagon |
| 1641. Yes | 1701. ¼ | 1761. A hexagon |
| 1642. A whole number | 1702. ¾ | 1762. A heptagon |
| 1643. 4 | 1703. ½ | 1763. An octagon |
| 1644. 1 | 1704. 0 | 1764. A nonagon |
| 1645. 0 | 1705. 3.280 | 1765. A decagon |
| 1646. Division | 1706. 4.9 | 1766. Octopus |
| 1647. Yes, to 2/5 | 1707. 4.80 | 1767. An octagon |
| 1648. Yes | 1708. 3.300 | 1768. A rhombus |
| 1649. ¼ | 1709. 3.500 | 1769. Congruent |
| 1650. 2/3 | 1710. 3.250 | 1770. Similar |
| 1651. Mixed | 1711. 6 | 1771. Symmetrical |
| 1652. 2 and 2/5 | 1712. Yes | 1772. Its center |
| 1653. Multiply 4x6 plus 1 over 4 | 1713. 1.8 | 1773. Area |
| 1654. 14/3 | 1714. Decimal points | 1774. 32 centimeters |
| 1655. 6 | 1715. A zero | 1775. 9 feet |
| 1656. 6 | 1716. 7 | 1776. Yes |
| 1657. 4 | 1717. 2.9 | 1777. 144 inches |
| 1658. Adding the numerators | 1718. 5 | 1778. Square foot, acre, square mile |
| 1659. 4/5 | 1719. .9 centimeters | 1779. Square centimeter, square meter, hectare, square kilometer |
| 1660. 12/9 | 1720. Equal to | |
| 1661. 10/10 or 1 | 1721. Geometry | 1780. 2 dimensional |
| 1662. 1 and 1/3 | 1722. A line | 1781. Yes |
| 1663. 4/7 | 1723. Letters | 1782. A prism |
| 1664. Find LCM first | 1724. An arrow | 1783. A cylinder |
| 1665. 5/6 | 1725. A ray | 1784. A pyramid |
| 1666. Find LCM first | 1726. The end point | 1785. A sphere |
| 1667. 1/3 | 1727. An angle | 1786. A cube |
| 1668. 4/9 | 1728. The vertex | 1787. A cone |
| 1669. 1 and ½ | 1729. Three | 1788. The surface area |
| 1670. 2 and 2/3 | 1730. A right angle | 1789. Yes |
| 1671. 2 feet | 1731. 90 degrees | 1790. The volume |
| 1672. ½ foot | 1732. Acute | 1791. 12 |
| 1673. 6 inches | 1733. Obtuse | 1792. No |
| 1674. Less than | 1734. Yes | 1793. A compass |
| 1675. Equal to | 1735. Isosceles | 1794. Radius |
| 1676. Equal to | 1736. Equilateral | 1795. Diameter |
| 1677. Yes | 1737. Scalene | 1796. Chord |
| 1678. ¼, 1/3, ½, and 1 | 1738. Right | 1797. The diameter |
| 1679. 1/8, ¼, ½, and 1 | 1739. A protractor | 1798. The radius |
| 1680. ½ | 1740. 50 degrees | 1799. 16 cm (D=Rx2) |
| 1681. ¼ | 1741. 180 degrees | 1800. Its circumference |
| 1682. 1 and ½ | 1742. 90 degrees | 1801. Yes |
| 1683. 2/9 | 1743. 270 degrees | 1802. Blue |
| 1684. 2/10 or 1/5 | 1744. 360 degrees | |
| 1685. ¼ | 1745. Intersecting | |

1803. 4
1804. Divide by the total numbers
1805. 4
1806. 8

1807. The median
1808. 4
1809. The mode
1810. 3
1811. The median

1812. 3
1813. The range
1814. 5

## Math – 5<sup>th</sup> Grade

1815. A billion
1816. A comma
1817. Three
1818. 5
1819. 6
1820. 7
1821. 8
1822. 9
1823. 612,000,000,000
1824. 5,480
1825. 53,927
1826. One thousand + one hundred + forty + five
1827. 9 Billion
1828. 800 Million
1829. 70 Million
1830. 6 Million
1831. 500 Thousand
1832. 40 Thousand
1833. 3 Thousand
1834. 2 Hundred
1835. Tens
1836. Ones
1837. Outlines; Dates, etc.
1838. 5
1839. 10
1840. 50
1841. 100
1842. 500
1843. 1000
1844. 1526
1845. 76
1846. 1686
1847. MMMV
1848. Digit to the right
1849. Yes
1850. 5
1851. 10 Million
1852. 9 Million
1853. 3,900,000
1854. 3,400,000
1855. 3,950,000
1856. 3,420,000
1857. 3000
1858. 2000
1859. 60,000
1860. 45,000
1861. 46,000
1862. 45,500
1863. 45,600

1864. 5,530
1865. 5,590
1866. 420
1867. 430
1868. Odd
1869. Even
1870. Even
1871. Odd
1872. Integers
1873. Yes
1874. Greater than
1875. Yes
1876. Opposite
1877. Gain value
1878. Lose value
1879. Positive number
1880. Negative number
1881. Positive
1882. Negative
1883. A minus
1884. No
1885. Opposites
1886. 5
1887. -7 (Negative seven)
1888. 20
1889. +10
1890. +25
1891. -5
1892. +10
1893. -15
1894. -200
1895. -4
1896. Less than
1897. Less than
1898. Greater than
1899. Greater than
1900. Less than
1901. Greater than
1902. Yes
1903. A positive
1904. To the right
1905. Negative
1906. To the left
1907. 6
1908. Yes
1909. -5
1910. -4
1911. -40
1912. 5
1913. Yes

1914. 10 + (-6)
1915. -6
1916. 0
1917. 0
1918. Yes
1919. Yes
1920. Adding its opposite
1921. Yes
1922. -2
1923. -3
1924. 6
1925. Yes
1926. Itself
1927. 4
1928. Yes
1929. 9
1930. Yes
1931. 2
1932. 3
1933. 4
1934. 5
1935. 6
1936. 7
1937. 36
1938. 49
1939. 8
1940. 81
1941. 100
1942. 12
1943. Exponents
1944. Small number raised up
1945. 2x2x2=8
1946. 5 cubed
1947. 5 to the fourth power
1948. 9
1949. 1000
1950. Yes
1951. 6
1952. One million
1953. 10 to the 9<sup>th</sup> power
1954. A prime number
1955. Composite numbers
1956. A composite number
1957. A prime number
1958. Composite numbers
1959. Prime
1960. Factors
1961. 1,2,4,8, and 16
1962. 2
1963. 3x3

| | | |
|---|---|---|
| **1964.** 3 to the second power | **2024.** 180 | **2082.** 2 |
| **1965.** 3x5 | **2025.** Greater than | **2083.** 90 |
| **1966.** 1,2,4,5,10, and 20 | **2026.** Equal to | **2084.** Turn it upside down |
| **1967.** 3 | **2027.** .21 | **2085.** 5/2 |
| **1968.** 2 | **2028.** 1 | **2086.** ¾ |
| **1969.** 9 | **2029.** 80 | **2087.** 2/3 |
| **1970.** 6 | **2030.** 23.25 | **2088.** 3/3 or 1 |
| **1971.** 24 | **2031.** 2 | **2089.** 7/9 |
| **1972.** Yes | **2032.** 232.5 | **2090.** 1 and 3/7 |
| **1973.** 21,000 | **2033.** $5.60 | **2091.** 4/3 |
| **1974.** The commutative | **2034.** 9,000 | **2092.** 1 and 1/3 |
| **1975.** The associative | **2035.** 2,000,000 | **2093.** 3 |
| **1976.** Less than | **2036.** Equal to | **2094.** 6 and 2/3 |
| **1977.** Equal to | **2037.** Division | **2095.** 4 and ½ |
| **1978.** Greater than | **2038.** The dividend | **2096.** 15 and ½ |
| **1979.** 400 | **2039.** The divisor | **2097.** Yes |
| **1980.** Yes | **2040.** The quotient | **2098.** 2/5 |
| **1981.** 3.3 | **2041.** 22 | **2099.** 3/8 |
| **1982.** .50 | **2042.** 12 | **2100.** 1 and 3/5 |
| **1983.** Yes | **2043.** 11 | **2101.** Yes |
| **1984.** Greater than | **2044.** 400 | **2102.** 3 |
| **1985.** Yes | **2045.** The remainder | **2103.** 3 |
| **1986.** Yes | **2046.** Yes | **2104.** Greater than |
| **1987.** Greater than | **2047.** Yes | **2105.** Equal to |
| **1988.** Zero | **2048.** Equal to | **2106.** Less than |
| **1989.** .8 | **2049.** 3 | **2107.** 3 |
| **1990.** 4 inches | **2050.** 10 | **2108.** 6 |
| **1991.** Algebra | **2051.** 1 | **2109.** Yes |
| **1992.** A letter | **2052.** 48.34 | **2110.** Yes |
| **1993.** The variable | **2053.** 2 | **2111.** The commutative |
| **1994.** .3 | **2054.** 4.834 | **2112.** 3 |
| **1995.** Equal to | **2055.** Numerator and Denominator | **2113.** Yes |
| **1996.** 15 | **2056.** The bottom | **2114.** Goodbye |
| **1997.** Subtraction | **2057.** The top | **2115.** 1/15 |
| **1998.** Inverse | **2058.** 2/8 | **2116.** 4/15 |
| **1999.** 12-5=7 | **2059.** ½ | **2117.** 1/8 |
| **2000.** 14+8=22 | **2060.** 2/3 | **2118.** 4/15 |
| **2001.** Yes | **2061.** 6 | **2119.** 30 |
| **2002.** 39 | **2062.** Find the least common multiple | **2120.** 10 |
| **2003.** 900 | **2063.** 6 | **2121.** 14 |
| **2004.** 101,000 | **2064.** 6 | **2122.** Yes |
| **2005.** $2.50 | **2065.** 2 | **2123.** 5 |
| **2006.** $26.00 | **2066.** 4/5 | **2124.** 1 |
| **2007.** Equal to | **2067.** 5 | **2125.** 3 |
| **2008.** 30 | **2068.** An integer and a fraction | **2126.** 1 and ½ |
| **2009.** $800 | **2069.** 1 and 1/3 | **2127.** 1 |
| **2010.** Yes | **2070.** Less than | **2128.** The ratio |
| **2011.** 72 | **2071.** Common denominator | **2129.** 1:3 (One to three) |
| **2012.** Add | **2072.** Yes | **2130.** 2:5 (2 to 5) |
| **2013.** 10,000 | **2073.** 15 | **2131.** ¼ |
| **2014.** 42,000 | **2074.** 10/15 | **2132.** 25% |
| **2015.** 350,000 | **2075.** 2/3 | **2133.** 50% |
| **2016.** Yes | **2076.** 12/15 | **2134.** 75% |
| **2017.** Commutative | **2077.** 4/5 | **2135.** Yes |
| **2018.** Associative | **2078.** 4/5 | **2136.** 2 to 1 |
| **2019.** Distributive | **2079.** ¼, 1/3, ½ ¾, and 1 | **2137.** 2 to 4 |
| **2020.** Distributive | **2080.** 1/24 | **2138.** Yes |
| **2021.** Zero | **2081.** 3/7 | **2139.** Unit rate |
| **2022.** Identity | | **2140.** 6 |
| **2023.** 120 | | **2141.** 25 cents per gumball |

2142. A ratio
2143. Yes
2144. 20 miles
2145. 6 to 1
2146. 1 to 6
2147. 1 to 10
2148. The rate
2149. Yes
2150. (65) miles per hour
2151. Miles
2152. Kilometers
2153. Distance
2154. 60 miles per hour
2155. Yes
2156. 100
2157. Century, Centimeter, etc.
2158. 30 out of 100
2159. 30/100 or 3/10
2160. 25%
2161. 50%
2162. 75%
2163. 100%
2164. ½
2165. ¾
2166. ¼
2167. 1
2168. .75
2169. .25
2170. .50
2171. 25%
2172. 25%
2173. 6/10
2174. Multiply
2175. 40
2176. 24
2177. $32
2178. Probability
2179. Yes
2180. 1 in 6
2181. Million
2182. 1 in 3
2183. 3 to 1
2184. ¼
2185. 25%
2186. .25
2187. The average
2188. 9 seconds
2189. 80%
2190. Mean
2191. 3
2192. Mode
2193. 15
2194. Median
2195. Order them by value
2196. 2,3,5,7,9
2197. 5
2198. Range
2199. 6
2200. Growth pattern
2201. 10

2202. 15
2203. 29
2204. Yes
2205. 4
2206. Yes
2207. Pictograph
2208. Yes
2209. Line plots
2210. Yes
2211. Yes
2212. A bar graph
2213. A line graph
2214. A pie chart
2215. A pie chart
2216. A bar graph
2217. A line graph
2218. A pictograph
2219. A survey
2220. Favorite color, food, etc.
2221. Algebra
2222. Variables
2223. 4
2224. 9
2225. 5
2226. Variables
2227. 19
2228. 1
2229. 4x4
2230. 4x4x4
2231. 16
2232. 3
2233. U.S. customary and Metric
2234. Pound
2235. Ounce, pound, ton
2236. 16
2237. 33 ounces
2238. 2000
2239. 1000
2240. 500
2241. 3000 pounds
2242. 12
2243. 3
2244. 1 yard
2245. Gram
2246. Milligram, gram, kilogram, metric ton
2247. 100
2248. Centigram
2249. 1000
2250. 2
2251. 1
2252. Liter
2253. 1
2254. Inch, foot, yard, mile
2255. Millimeter, Centimeter, meter, kilometer
2256. One meter
2257. A meter
2258. One foot

2259. 13 inches
2260. One inch
2261. Centimeter
2262. Millimeter
2263. One mile
2264. One kilometer
2265. Fahrenheit
2266. Celsius
2267. 0
2268. 100
2269. 212
2270. 98.6
2271. Fluid ounce, cup, pint, quart, gallon
2272. 4
2273. 2
2274. 16
2275. 24
2276. Acres
2277. 4
2278. Bushel
2279. 4
2280. Barrels
2281. Gallons
2282. Liter
2283. Milliliter, centiliter, liter, kiloliter
2284. A quart
2285. One yard
2286. One mile
2287. Says time
2288. 11.45
2289. Eastern
2290. States time zone
2291. Yes
2292. 11:35
2293. 1:00
2294. A.M.
2295. P.M.
2296. Before
2297. After
2298. Midnight
2299. 60 seconds
2300. 120
2301. 60
2302. 180 minutes
2303. 24 hours
2304. 48 hours
2305. 3 days
2306. 12 hours
2307. 6 hours
2308. 18 hours
2309. 28 days
2310. 12 weeks
2311. 6 months
2312. 365 ¼ days
2313. 365 ¼ days
2314. 52 weeks
2315. 366

2316. Leap year day every 4 years
2317. February 29th
2318. 10 years
2319. 100 years
2320. 200 years
2321. Yes
2322. Geometry
2323. Pencil or pen
2324. A line segment
2325. A line
2326. Ray
2327. It has an arrow
2328. Parallel
2329. Perpendicular
2330. Intersecting
2331. Symmetrical
2332. An intersection
2333. The vertex
2334. Protractor
2335. Degrees
2336. 360 degrees
2337. 180 degrees
2338. 90 degrees
2339. 90 degrees
2340. Yes
2341. 45 degrees
2342. Acute
2343. Obtuse
2344. A straight angle
2345. Reflex

2346. Greater than
2347. 180 degrees
2348. 60 degrees
2349. 90 degrees
2350. Polygons
2351. Circle, square, triangle, etc.
2352. 3
2353. Tricycle, trio, trilogy, etc.
2354. Equilateral
2355. Isosceles
2356. Scalene
2357. Right
2358. 45 degrees
2359. Congruent
2360. Equilateral
2361. The hypotenuse
2362. ½ Base x Height
2363. A quadrilateral
2364. A rectangle
2365. Width x Height
2366. Length of side squared
2367. 25 Centimeters
2368. Square
2369. A trapezoid
2370. A parallelogram
2371. Parallelograms
2372. A square
2373. Two
2374. Square can be rectangle
2375. A pentagon

2376. A hexagon
2377. A heptagon
2378. An octagon
2379. A nonagon
2380. A decagon
2381. Width x height
2382. 24 feet
2383. A circle
2384. Compass
2385. 360 degrees
2386. A chord
2387. Diameter
2388. The diameter
2389. The radius
2390. Circumference
2391. Greek pi $\pi$
2392. Its diameter
2393. 3.14
2394. March 14th
2395. Solid figures
2396. Solid figures
2397. Cone, sphere, pyramid, etc.
2398. Three-dimensional
2399. 6
2400. Yes
2401. Length x width x height
2402. 24 inches
2403. Mathematics
2404. Arithmetic
2405. States favorite math

# Bibliography

"Ducksters: Education Site for Kids and Teachers." *Ducksters: Education Site for Kids and Teachers*. N.p., n.d. Web. Accessed 2014. http://www.ducksters.com.

"ENCHANTED LEARNING HOME PAGE." *ENCHANTED LEARNING HOME PAGE*. N.p., n.d. Web. 10 Accessed 2014. http://www.enchantedlearning.com.

"Fact Monster from Information Please." *Fact Monster: Online Almanac, Dictionary, Encyclopedia, and Homework Help*. N.p., n.d. Web. Accessed 2014. http://www.factmonster.com.

Grade Level Help at Internet 4 Classrooms." *Grade Level Help at Internet 4 Classrooms*. N.p., n.d. Web. Accessed 2014. http://www.internet4classrooms.com.

Hirsch, E. D. *What Your First grader Needs to Know: Fundamentals of a Good First-Grade Education*. New York: Doubleday, 1991. Print.

Hirsch, E. D. *What Your Third Grader Needs to Know: Fundamentals of a Good Third-Grade Education*. New York: Doubleday, 1992. Print.

Hirsch, E. D. *What Your Fourth Grader Needs to Know: Fundamentals of a Good Fourth-Grade Education*. New York: Doubleday, 1992. Print.

Hirsch, E. D. *What Your Fifth Grader Needs to Know: Fundamentals of a Good Fifth-Grade Education*. New York: Doubleday, 1993. Print.

Hirsch, E. D., and John Holdren. *What Your Kindergartner Needs to Know: Preparing Your Child for a Lifetime of Learning*. New York: Doubleday, 1996. Print.

Hirsch, E. D. *What Your Second Grader Needs to Know: Fundamentals of a Good Second-Grade Education*. Rev. Ed. New York: Dell, 1998. Print.

Hirsch, E. D., and Linda Bevilacqua. *What Your Preschooler Needs to Know*. New York, NY: Bantam Dell, 2008. Print.

"K-12 Curriculum." *Cedarburg*. N.p., n.d. Web. June 2014. http://www.cedarburg.buildyourowncurriculum.com/public/Landing_Grades.aspx.

"Make an Amazing Timeline in Minutes." *Preceden: Timeline Maker & Timeline Generator*. N.p., n.d. Web. Accessed 2014. http://www.preceden.com.

"Native Indian Tribes." *Warpaths2piecepipes*. N.p., n.d. Web. Accessed 2014. http://www.warpaths2piecepipes.com.

# BIBLIOGRAPHY

"Typical Course of Study." *Typical Course of Study*. N.p., n.d. Web. 10 July 2014.
    http://www.worldbook.com/typical-course-of-study.

"Online Dictionary | Thesaurus." *Online Dictionary*. N.p., n.d. Web. Accessed 2014.
    http://www.onlinedictionary.com.

"Practice Math & Language Arts." *IXL Math and English*. N.p., n.d. Web. Accessed 2014. http://www.ixl.com.

"The Great Idea Finder - Celebrating the Spirit of Innovation." *The Great Idea Finder - Celebrating the Spirit of Innovation*. N.p., n.d. Web. Accessed 2014. http://www.ideafinder.com.

"Top Ten Lists at TheTopTens." *Top Ten Lists at TheTopTens*. N.p., n.d. Web. Accessed 2014.
    http://www.thetoptens.com.

"Touropia - Travel, Tours and Top Tens." *Touropia*. N.p., n.d. Web. Accessed 2014. http://www.touropia.com.

"Wikepedia.com." *Wikepedia.com*. N.p., n.d. Web. 30 Accessed 2014. http://www.wikepedia.com.

www.ingramcontent.com/pod-product-compliance
Lightning Source LLC
Chambersburg PA
CBHW081255040426
42452CB00014B/2512